THE
PHILOSOPHY
CURE

Prescription:

THE PHILOSOPHY CURE

Lessons on Living

from the

Great Philosophers

LAURENCE DEVILLAIRS

Translated by Jesse Browner

ST. MARTIN'S
ESSENTIALS
NEW YORK

Published in the United States by St. Martin's Essentials,
an imprint of St. Martin's Publishing Group

THE PHILOSOPHY CURE. Copyright © 2020 by Laurence Devillairs.
Translation © 2020 by Jesse Browner. All rights reserved.
Printed in the United States of America. For information, address
St. Martin's Publishing Group, 120 Broadway, New York, N.Y. 10271.

www.stmartins.com

Designed by Steven Seighman

Library of Congress Cataloging-in-Publication Data

Names: Devillairs, Laurence, author. | Browner, Jesse, translator.
Title: The philosophy cure : lessons on living from the great philosophers /
    Laurence Devillairs ; translated by Jesse Browner.
Other titles: Guérir la vie par la philosophie. English
Description: First U.S. edition. | New York : St. Martin's Essentials, 2020. |
    Includes bibliographical references and index.
Identifiers: LCCN 2019048695 | ISBN 9781250759887 (trade paperback) |
    ISBN 9781250237705 (ebook)
Subjects: LCSH: Conduct of life. | Life. | Ethics. | Philosophy.
Classification: LCC BJ1590 .D4813 2020 | DDC 170/.44—dc23
LC record available at https://lccn.loc.gov/2019048695

Our books may be purchased in bulk for promotional, educational,
or business use. Please contact your local bookseller or the
Macmillan Corporate and Premium Sales Department at 1-800-221-7945,
extension 5442, or by email at MacmillanSpecialMarkets@macmillan.com.

Originally published in France by Universitaires de France/Humensis, 2017

First U.S. Edition: April 2020

10 9 8 7 6 5 4 3 2 1

For PG

There are no diseases; there are only the sick.

—Georges Canguilhem, *The Normal and the Pathological*

We can only think of Plato and Aristotle in grand academic robes. They were honest men, like others, laughing with their friends, and when they diverted themselves with writing their *Laws* and the *Politics*, they did it as an amusement. That part of their life was the least philosophic and the least serious; the most philosophic was to live simply and quietly. If they wrote on politics, it was as if laying down rules for a lunatic asylum.

—Blaise Pascal, *Pensées*, 331[1]

CONTENTS

Introduction   1

Use as Directed: Healing Your Life   4

AFFLICTIONS OF THE BODY

Beautiful, Fat, Ugly, and Skinny   21

The Last Act Is Tragic   26

Nothing Is More Despicable Than Illness   31

Suffering   37

Aging   41

Tobacco, Alcohol, and Addiction   45

Hunger: The Dietetics of Pleasure   51

Afflictions of the Brain   56

AFFLICTIONS OF THE SOUL

Living   65

Daily Life   69

Akrasia, or the Counterfeit Disease   74

Burnout   79

Good Company, Bad Company: "Man Is Wolf to Man"   84

Fear and Trembling   88

Love   93

Love at First Sight   99

Opium Smokers   102

Regrets and Remorse   106

THE WORRIES OF EVERYDAY LIFE

Money 115

Neighborhood Problems 120

The Bore, the Pygmalion, and the Soliloquist 123

(Other People's) Children, Friends, and Family 126

Bosses and Colleagues 129

*Getting Wet at the Pool, and Other Things
    You Can't Change* 133

AFFLICTIONS OF THE MIND, TEMPORARY AND CHRONIC

Depression, Melancholy, Taedium Vitae, or Acedia 141

Envy, Jealousy, and Schadenfreude 145

LIFE'S LITTLE ACCIDENTS

Mistakes, Sins, and a Guilty Conscience 153

Failure, Defeat, and Bankruptcy 159

BORDERLINE CASES

Identity Disorders: Shame and Narcissism 167

Madness 170

Solitude and Isolation 173

Suicide 175

CURIOUS THEORIES

Sports Make You Antisocial 181

Gathering No Moss 184

Man Is a Hunting Dog Like Any Other 186

Growing Plants and Perfume 189

Pedantry and Donkey's Milk   191
Happiness in the Moment Is the Happiness of a Cow   193
The Transitional Object   195
Learning to Understand Love by Watching Comedies   197
Animal Philosophies   199

Acknowledgments   203
Notes   205
Index of Authors Cited   223
About the Author   225

THE
PHILOSOPHY
CURE

INTRODUCTION

It's Not All Fun and Games

TO HEAR SOME people tell it, the secret of happiness is to live your life, feel alive, and exist in the here and now. As if life were a gift, as if the present moment were nothing but magic and poetry. That may be true for those who live on love and fresh water, vacations and leisure, luxury, serenity, and self-indulgence. For most of us, however, life is not a gift but a series of imposed constraints, calculations, and schedules. Not because of the daily grind of commuting, working, and sleeping but, above all, because life is made up of a whole series of things that we have not, or have only partially, chosen for ourselves: our body, our personality, the era we live in, our address, our neighbors, our routine, the conditions in which we perform our work. Living almost never involves beginning; more often than not, it is merely a matter of accepting and persisting. In most matters, we make do rather than choose. Our freedom is not absolute, without compulsion or limits. It adapts, finding its own place in an environment that existed long before we came along and that we did not design.

Living means suffering. In "A Litany," the sixteenth-century English poet John Donne asked God to ensure that "our affections kill us not, nor dye."[1] This poetic prayer encapsulates the plight in which we, the living, find ourselves: we are incapable of not seeking our own happiness, love, and success; but anything we desire can also undo us, because everything is at once both essential and ephemeral, because nothing is predictable, because everything is irreversible and suffering is not a weed that we can simply uproot. Life isn't all fun and games. So how can philosophy be of use to us in the hard work of existing? Can it help us to survive the very thing that kills us even as it expires?

Philosophy is useful; it is neither a luxury nor an occupation for dilettantes. It does not exalt the utility of anything that is useless or the felicity of anything that serves no purpose; on the contrary, philosophy thinks no thought that is not useful. And that utility is of a dual nature: it can either provide those of us who suffer various ills with diagnoses and expertise, or it can teach those of us who believe ourselves to be in good health that we are, in fact, ill. In the latter case, without philosophy the illness may go undetected and the infection may spread. As a particular form of biopsy, the philosophical examination reveals what neither the doctor nor the psychologist nor we ourselves are capable of detecting. As a balm for our wounds—romantic breakups, trouble with the neighbors, professional failures, weariness of life—philosophy can be seen as a branch of medicine like any other, with its own repository of unguents and sedatives. But it is unparalleled as a means of unmasking a problem that we do not understand even as we endure its secondary effects. Who but the philosopher can tell us how to prevent our affections both from killing us and from dying? We have two options: either we are sick and ask philosophy to propose a treatment, or else we believe that we are healthy and philosophy must convince us of the contrary, thereby offering us true health and true healing.

All philosophy lays claim to the status of medicine, although some philosophers do so more loudly and emphatically than others, such as the ancient Greeks, Epicureans, or Stoics, for whom "Vain is the word of that philosopher who can ease no mortal trouble,"[2] or Nietzsche, who claims for himself the status of doctor of culture. The diagnoses vary, as do the suggested cures, but the goal remains the same: to identify what's wrong, be it grief or gangrene, whatever prevents a person from being herself or obtaining her due, be it happiness or the truth. There is something orthopedic about philosophy, as if we all have the ability to walk but suffer from some sprain, vertigo, or motor defect. We can neither abjure our desire for truth and happiness nor satisfy it. Lame and clumsy, we are at one and the same time capable and incapable, desirous and unsatisfied—in a word, we are sick. We do not measure up to our own ambitions; we do not enjoy the health to which we aspire. So it's not merely the ideas that are to be found at the intersection of medicine and morality, matters of bioethics, that inform philosophy as a branch of medicine; nor is it because some philosophers have been doctors or anatomists. It is because life itself is a disease of which we must be cured.

USE AS DIRECTED

Healing Your Life

PHILOSOPHY DOES NOT kill; it makes us stronger. It even has the power to cure. But the question is knowing what it is that we are being cured of. The desired goal seems easy enough to define: we want to be healthy. But is it our bodies or our minds that we want to be healthy, or both? What do we call the kind of health that the philosophy cure supposedly offers us: Happiness? Wisdom? Consolation? Normalcy? Do we seek relief from temporary discomfort or do we hope to be delivered from some deeper-rooted evil?

Kierkegaard entitled his most definitive book *The Sickness Unto Death*. In other words, he claims to be addressing a disease that ends only in death, and which he identifies as despair. From cradle to grave, we are dying of despair. It is therefore philosophy's job to cure us of "the greatest spiritual sickness,"[1] which is the death in life embodied by despair. To live is either to despair or to dare to be oneself. There is no in-between, because no one who carries the disease is free of its symptoms. We must decide between despair and the courage to be ourselves.

Does this mean that all the diseases that we might treat with philosophy are fatal, critically serious, and exclusively psychic? If that were the case, wouldn't we have a better chance of being cured by psychology, psychiatry, or neurobiology than by philosophy? Who do we turn to—the doctor, the psychologist, or the philosopher? The most prudent answer would certainly seem to be that the one does not exclude the other, that the remedies proposed by one discipline do not prevent us from trying out those of the others. A bolder response would be to confront the objection head-on and ask whether the therapeutic function of philosophy is not a purely metaphorical one, with no real power to cure. But isn't it a kind of scientism to believe that only those diseases that we treat with science are real? Isn't it scientism, too, to reduce all existential questions to the realm of psychology, to view our anxieties as mere expressions of temperament and our confusions as a sign of dysfunction that can be fixed with solid clinical and psychical reeducation?

The diagnoses offered by philosophy may be seen as flawed because they are weighed down by the Great Questions—What is Man? What is Life? What is Freedom?—and too abstract to be real. If we reject them, however, we run the risk of reducing the individual to the sum of her behaviors and of seeing her only from the outside, based on her actions. But we are more than merely what we do; our behavior does not reveal all that we are. We also need to account for what can't be seen—our motives, our intentions, our desires—all of which we can just as easily betray as fulfill through our actions.

We cannot set aside our inner life, the ebb and flow of our feelings, our thoughts, our reflections, the perpetual restlessness that plagues us and whose influence is just as powerful as that of our behavior. None of this can be reduced to the psychological or the psychosomatic; rather, it's the signature of every individual's singular manner of living and what makes our own experience unique to each of us. It all adds up to the fact that only I can be me, that I alone have what it takes to be me.

Know Thyself

It was philosophy that gave a name to that part of every individual that can be ascribed to her physiology or psyche without being reduced to it—the unique place that belongs to each person. Philosophy was born out of this process of geolocalization. Indeed, one sunny day in Delphi, Socrates, one of the inventors of the discipline, was suddenly struck by the aphorism "Know thyself." Although it is neither scientific nor medical, knowing yourself is the prescription of choice in the philosopher's own scientific and medical practice. "Who am I?" is a question for philosophy. And an answer. It launched a reign that continues to this day—the reign of the soul. For it is to the soul that the injunction to know yourself is addressed. Only the soul can secure such knowledge, and it is only because each of us has a soul that this recommendation can be made. Asking myself who I am makes sense only because I am a soul.[2] It's not about going off in search of your capacities; of knowing your own character, biases, and preferences, but about concerning yourself with what is essential. Philosophy is not religion just because it speaks of the soul and the care it requires. On the contrary, it is through the knowledge of yourself as a soul that its specific powers are best expressed; philosophy speaks of the soul because it alone is capable of knowing the soul and of understanding the demands of having one.

And the soul is demanding. We can lose it; neglect it; or, contrarily, know it and watch over it. That is how it endows our being with momentum, history, and prospective experience. For human beings, existence isn't in the order of a given; quite the opposite, it's something that can be subject to modification and made into theater. Having a soul makes the business of living not only a question ("Who am I?") but also a prescription—we never merely *are*; we *have to be*. We have to be the person that our soul requires us to be. So "Know thyself" also means "Be the person you have to be," "Be the soul you know yourself to be." In other words, until proven otherwise, we are the only creatures that do not take their own existence for granted, whose existence is a whole complicated saga. Not only because we act, make choices, and take decisions but also because, for us, being is never just a fact but a calling, a duty, a goal. Because being is not a self-evident, hassle-free state but the source of innate anxiety: Who must I be? Who can I hope to be?

We are more than just the condition of becoming, changing at the whim of events and encounters with the passage of time. We are not merely a story that ravels and unfolds; our existence is not an inventory of everything our relationships and environment have made of us. There is in us a primordial solitude that makes each of us alone in being ourselves and ensures that, whatever we may do or want, each of us is only our self. Nobody exists in my stead and I cannot exist in anyone else's stead. Existence is the only thing we cannot exchange or delegate, and the soul is nothing but the necessity of owning our own existence.

That doesn't mean that we are transparent to ourselves or that there is no mystery in being ourselves. On the contrary, the soul is more of an enigma than an ID. It's an arena of conflict and a source of guesswork, and being ourselves has more in common with bull-fighting than with classical ballet. The landscapes of our soul, its "plains and caves, and caverns of my memory,"[3] are largely unknown to us, its truths unsuspected or unstable—making sincerity a highly perilous undertaking. We can't even be certain that we are made to have just one soul, just one "me." We are nothing but one "great riddle"[4] to ourselves. That's because we're looking at it the wrong way; we're looking at ourselves much too up close to see ourselves as we are. That's why, more often than not, our actions seem ambiguous or outright strange ("Why did I do that?"), as do the contradictions that we struggle to overcome ("I didn't want to do it, but the urge was stronger than I am."). One of the key functions of the philosophy cure is, precisely, to end the wars raging within us, to establish peace on the battlefield that is us. Traditionally, the armed struggle is waged between the soul and the passions that besiege and enslave it; both ancient and classical philosophy—from Seneca to Spinoza and even Kant in the eighteenth century—view the passions of anger, love, and vanity as the prime diseases of the soul.

The great riddle that I am to myself, and which philosophy seeks to solve, is not an intellectual game or a mere problem of logic; it sets out a life choice. What kind of life must I lead to be who I am? It's not only a question of knowing ourselves; it's also a question of living. What is the best life, the one best suited to who I am? "Our debate is upon a question which has the highest conceivable claims to the serious interest even of a person who has but little intelligence—namely, what course of life is best."[5]

The Courage to Exist

So it would seem that Kierkegaard was right. It's not enough to merely live—we need to heal life. That is the very particular condition that philosophy is designed to treat. That is where its utility and profound originality lie: it does not deliver instructions; it does not prescribe behaviors; and it does not cure dysfunctions. It cures life, the very fact of having to live. Philosophy must not be treated like a leisure activity, to be squeezed in between gardening and the book club; as I said earlier, it's more like bullfighting, in that it requires the courage to face up to all that is brutal and dangerous in the very act of living. It's not about abandoning ourselves to life's sweet pleasures but about climbing down into the ring and sidling up as close as possible to the very thing that would crush us. While there may be no beauty to be found in a bullfight—that brightly colored butcher's dance of twirling arms, legs, and garish costumes—life itself is not much better, hard as we may try to veil its stark and glaring realities in a cloak of dreams and make-believe.

It's not the philosopher's job to live well or to live badly; it's her job to reveal all that is obscure about life. Philosophy, therefore, is no abstract activity cut off from real life. At the same time, it has the troubling and confounding power of turning things we take for granted into problems—like how to live, for instance. The truth is, how to live is a question that we usually don't ask ourselves, because our daily routine is governed by the need for haste and a lack of time. At any given moment, I find myself having to make decisions both trivial and consequential; I have to make the best of situations that are not of my own making, with no time to pull myself together or even to pause for a reset. There's no way to seize the high ground over existence, to set ourselves aside or above the field so as to ensure the soundness of our judgment. We are required to reflect, to decide, and to act all at the same time. The paradox of daily life is that it is both humdrum and hair-trigger, never fully alien but changing from moment to moment. Life rushes along . . . to live. Is there anything philosophy can do to help with this problem?

Boldness. That is the Cartesian way—to live well, we must live to the full. With a generosity directed first and foremost at ourselves. We have to see the big picture, reach wide, not measure our lives out by the thimbleful but be determined and resolute in all things. It is not so much about being proactive as about being bold, a combination of courage and risk-taking, a broad scope of vision and action, a sense of having conquered indecision, which, if Descartes is to be believed, is the worst of all evils. The generosity with which we act and live must have some excess to it. It takes more passion than moderation to nurture the ability to never sell yourself short. To persist and to own, to place the stamp of your will on everything you do. To see yourself in the choices you make, even when you fail, even when you go astray. The important thing is to measure up to all the decisions you make.

That is the only way to get anywhere, to avoid the "if I'd only known" and "if at least" moments that make us feel as if we are living in the margins of our own existence. It hardly matters what path you choose; the essential thing is to choose, "following the example of travelers, who, finding themselves lost in a forest, know that they ought not to wander first to one side and then to the other, nor, still less, to stop in one place, but understand that they should continue to walk as straight as they can in one direction, not diverging for any slight reason, even though it was possibly chance alone that first determined them in their choice."[6]

The Reality Test

It takes boldness to confront reality and carve out a livable space within it. Reality is neither a bed of roses nor a disaster, but impartially one and the other in turn, and it never truly belongs to us. It borrows unpredictability from the wheel of fortune and a fearsome irreversibility from the arrow of time. What is done cannot be undone and what happens happens without our ever being able to fully predict or alter it. We are thus forced to consent to that which does not ask for our consent and to accept that which gives us no other choice—that is the reality test. That is the life test. There is an order of things, be it fortuity or necessity, that eludes our agency, and is just as capable of obstructing it as of supporting it, of blessing it as of punishing it.

One of philosophy's great lessons, its dispensary or pharmacy, is to teach us that while we may not be masters of destiny, we are masters of ourselves and of the manner in which we deal with whatever comes our way. This master lesson was first taught by the Stoics, the heirs of Socrates, whose school survived more than five centuries and whose influence is still felt to this day. It's the vein that connects to Cartesian generosity. The principle of this course of treatment is a simple one: fear is fueled by fear, and not by the object of fear. Things are not tragic in and of themselves but because we deem them to be tragic. While we don't get to choose what happens, we do get to choose how much importance we attach to it and how we see it—sad, joyful, unbearable, or encouraging. This is the philosophical version of the glass half-full/glass half-empty polemic. The glass is what it is, but it's up to us to adjust our reading of it. In other words, if we perfect the way we evaluate things, our fears will disappear. If we want to stare into reality's eyes, we need to abandon the pointless worries and false hopes that prevent us from seeing things as they are.

The aim of this Stoical course of treatment is to shield us—we ourselves, our well-being, and our peace of mind—from external events and their random vagaries. Allowing your happiness to depend on the ups and downs of fortune is to live with heartburn and butterflies in your stomach. It's a good lesson. It requires courage, as we've seen, but also acceptance of everything that limits the extent of that courage and dims its brilliance. The world predates us and will outlive us; it imposes its own reality and constraints on all we do and are. The French phenomenological philosopher Maurice Merleau-Ponty put it this way: "It is true that we are always free to accept or refuse life. By accepting it we take the factual situations—our bodies, our faces, our way of being—upon ourselves; we accept our responsibilities, we sign a contract with the world and with men."[7] We accept reality and all its frustrating and unpredictable implications for our desires.

Yes, Socrates

We are tested by existence, tested by our daily routine, tested by reality. . . . When all is said and done, life can seem all but unlivable. Mightn't it be easier to just admit that we're not equipped to meet its challenges? Reality is here, in our face, hulking and mute, dismissing or granting our desires without judgment. In such circumstances, which are undeniably our own, the function of philosophy is above all aerodynamic—it is there to help us negotiate our relationship to reality just as we negotiate a bend in the road. Its role is not merely to cauterize old wounds or to calm fears of the future; it is our immediate suffering—all too concrete, cumbersome, and tormenting—that it must cure us of. And the discourse it adopts in doing so is no more incidental than the words a doctor uses when delivering her diagnosis.

And yet, what are we to make of a philosophical style that's more often than not embodied in weighty treatises or exhausted dialogues in which the adversary is reduced to muttering "Yes, Socrates," "Certainly, Socrates," to the point where we're almost embarrassed for him. But that's how philosophical medicine works—we're quickly disarmed by its words, as if all it takes is for Socrates to speak, for the philosopher to open his mouth, to silence our own chatter and reveal its frivolity and emptiness. Nothing can stand up against this new language, which I have never heard anywhere else, yet which speaks to me personally. It tells no story, it describes nothing, and yet something happens. Through their power to unsettle us, philosophical concepts bear the same weight as actions; they can be as surprising as events and demand equal attention. They leave us speechless because the questions posed by philosophy are ones we have never asked. That's the true meaning of "Yes, Socrates"—the interlocutor is not without intelligence or wit, but Socrates's discourse is so unconventional that his partner in dialogue cannot find the words to respond to it.

The style and talent of philosophy lie above all in laying out problems for which we have no ready-made solution at hand. We'd never thought of that before, we'd never even asked ourselves that question; and now along comes Socrates to put it into words and an entire field of possibilities we never imagined opens up. Philosophy must be an eminently nonconformist and iconoclastic activity. Its natural attitude must be one of cynicism, a school of thought from ancient Greece, directly descended from Socrates, that made this baffling and unexpected dimension of philosophical discourse so provocative.

Philosophy can claim to heal the afflictions of the body and the soul because it has the capacity to identify and eliminate the sources of their infection. It is a natural incubator of antibodies, the most famous of which is reason. Reason has been swatting at flies for centuries and draws its power from its ability to recognize and speak the truth. Because it embodies knowledge of the world, of humankind, and even of God, it is capable of defining all that is accessible, beneficial, and appropriate to us. But it administers its special medicine by dissolving our certainties. Thus, Socrates is a gadfly, a busybody who goes along diagnosing perfectly healthy people and ends up leaving them incurable and buried under a pile of their former convictions. What motivates the doctor-philosopher is not so much illness as our ignorance that we are ill; it's his certainty that there's something not right about humankind, some sort of latent, innate virus. The other branches of medicine do nothing more than apply bandages to a wooden leg; philosophy alone seeks to transform the very wood of which we are made, thereby making all the bandages contrived by others useless and ineffectual.

Toward a Philosophy of Cruelty

We have little use for this particular branch of medicine, which relies on reason and paradox to conclude, for instance, that pity is a form of fear, love is cannibalism, free will is an illusion, and servitude is always voluntary. We have our own recipes and magical remedies to pit against such philosophical therapy: "I shall be like a doctor tried by a bench of children on a charge brought by a cook,"[8] Socrates insists. Sick without knowing what we are sick of, we refuse to recognize ourselves in the portrait that the philosopher paints of us: "'A strange image you speak of . . . and strange prisoners,'" we complain to Socrates as he describes his famous cave dwellers. "'Like to us,'" he replies.[9] If philosophy is capable of healing, it certainly can't do so on the basis of consensus. If we didn't exaggerate it, truth would remain effectively unseen and we would have a hard time imagining it. There is indeed a kind of cruelty in philosophy that applies pressure precisely where it hurts, right on the sore spot that we had hoped to keep hidden away. This metaphysical cruelty has no qualms about abusing our mind, upsetting it in order to force it to seek further and deeper for the truth.

Antonin Artaud identified "metaphysics, the plague, cruelty"[10] as realms we have abandoned—out of cowardice? out of comfortable complacency?—but that we must return to.[11] If, as we insist, metaphysics has the power of revelation, it is because it "causes the mask to fall, reveals the lie, the slackness, baseness, and hypocrisy of our world; it shakes off the asphyxiating inertia of matter"[12] in which our thoughts and even our lives slumber. It must restore to language and thought "their power to shatter as well as really to manifest something."[13] Metaphysics is not a still life; it must make us uncomfortable, and if we feel not even a little pain in undergoing the arid cure of vigilance and reflection, it's because the remedy is weaker than the disease and no amount of philosophizing will help. Metaphysics is the only way to "again bring into fashion the great preoccupations and great essential passions"[14]—those dealing with the truth; good and evil; freedom and servitude; God, both in his existence and in his absence; all that vast realm of turmoil that we have psychologized and reduced to personality tests, to mere questions of temperament.

But philosophy is not psychology. Psychology is interested in the individual as she is acted upon and subjected to, at a remove from the determined and conditioned contexts of social status, religion, sexuality, generation. . . . It deals only with behaviors, functions, and dysfunctions. As the French philosopher and physician Georges Canguilhem wrote, "The fact is, many works of psychology seem to combine a philosophy without rigor with an ethic of laxity and medical treatment without controls."[15] If metaphysics ever returns to fashion, it will do so only by radically distinguishing itself from such medical treatment without controls; such lax morality; and such spineless, unrigorous psychology. The hour is dark but ours is not a desperate case, because for each of our afflictions there is a cure.

AFFLICTIONS
OF THE BODY

WE ARE READY to accept that philosophy is medicine for the soul and that its place and utility are therefore to be found somewhere between psychoanalysis and psychology, but we are more reluctant to admit that it can also cure our bodily afflictions or that it even has anything at all to do with the body. And yet that's probably where we are most in need of help. The body is totally visible and exposed, and for that reason constantly at risk of slipping into the realm of object. That is surely even more so for women, who are condemned to be their bodies—bodies that are certain to be objectified. One is not born a woman; one must grow into her likeness.

The physical is not forgiving; it can't be reasoned with and is hardly open to interpretation. When you suffer, you suffer. When you're ugly, you're ugly. The physical is the realm of Manichaeism and clear-cut opposites: pleasant, painful; pretty, hideous. The bastions of reality reject nuance—it's in your face, it is what it is, without mystery or veiled appearance. All is visible, and more or less immutable. Your weight, your height, your bones, and your flesh are subject to the faintest of consolations and the flimsiest of prostheses.

BEAUTIFUL, FAT, UGLY, AND SKINNY

THE TRUTH IS, we prefer beauty. Life is a big lottery, with its first drawing at birth—a lucky draw means you've inherited a face and a figure society deem pleasing; an unlucky draw gives you features verging on caricature. It's easy to understand why the ancient Greeks and Romans saw the divine Fates as the source of both good luck and of bad.

The fact is, before any direction has been taken or decision made, life starts out with a kind of sweepstakes in which we're deemed either attractive or ugly. We're stuck either with a burden or a windfall that we have neither sought nor earned. This is all the result of the absolute arbitrariness of our appearance and how society perceives it, the destiny of how we look—regardless of what we may choose to do.

Diagnosis

Five foot seven, 130 pounds, green eyes, brown hair—the first things to define us are numbers, measurements, colors, a shape, a body. Paradoxically, we're able to identify ourselves precisely by that which we have not chosen for ourselves. The thing that allows us to be recognized and differentiated from everyone else is the one thing we didn't ask for; our body, our face are both us and not us. They are us because we are as we appear—these eyes and these hands are indeed my own—and not us because we experience our physical appearance as something exterior that has been given to us and that we have neither created nor chosen—these eyes and hands are mine yet not me, not all of me. There is in us a primary material that preexists anything we might later do to mold it by diet, exercise, style, or surgery.

The cult of appearance is in fact a rejection of appearance. We do everything we can to transform this primary material, to make it less material and less primary, more sophisticated and somehow spiritual. We wear makeup because we want to turn our bodies and our faces into something that looks like who we are. So the body becomes enticement, our features become charms, our eyes become gaze, our face becomes expression. We never allow our body its own embodiment, our physique its own materiality. The cult of appearance is the cult of the soul, or of personality, of that part of the body that expresses what we are or what we want to be. We need to make our silent flesh speak and to adorn its nakedness.

Philosophical Therapy

What powers does philosophy have in this domain? Philosophy feels so . . . metaphysical, that is, explicitly above and beyond the physical. Some philosophers talk a good game about themselves, conjugate their ideas in the first person; but they never tell us what they look like.[1] That is one of the differences between literature and philosophy, which has little or no use for descriptions, personas, and portraits. "I was forty-five years old, my name was René Descartes, I had a strong nose, dark eyes a little too close together, thick hair, etc." There is nothing of the sort in the introduction to the *Meditations*. This great thinker about the relationship between the soul and the body says nothing about what it feels like inside René Descartes's skin, to have René Descartes's face, as if there were no philosophical interest in the physical. And yet Socrates claims to be just as concerned with hair and dirt as with ideas.[2] At the same time, the twentieth-century French philosopher Emmanuel Levinas develops an entire thesis around the face, a unique understanding of the other, and of the individual as well. But in his case the face has a moral status—it's the incarnation of the law that forbids us from killing our neighbor, be he friend or foe. It's the vessel in which that timeless commandment takes physical form and imposes itself on each of us. The face of another is in itself a precept and an injunction: "Thou shalt not kill." It is, for each of us, first and foremost the face of humanity. It's not the eyes, the forehead, the chin, or anything that makes up its physical attributes that we see when we look at a human face but, on the contrary, everything that makes it a moral principle and, ultimately, disembodied.[3]

We have to admit that this is no help to us in accepting our own physicality—or anyone else's, for that matter. No one ever presents himself to me as a disembodied, abstract, moral entity; he always has his own specific features and physiognomy, even his own smell. It is those characteristics that may be difficult to love or, contrarily, the objects of our passion, and not the face as an ethical law, requiring us to respect all of humankind in every human. Is there even one school of philosophy that explains what it means to look the way we look?

Derrida's Cat

We use more than just mascara, perfume, and other kinds of balm, to beautify ourselves; we do it with our clothing, to reveal or to conceal, and also with language. Talking gives life to your body, both to claim it as your own and to make it the object of other people's gaze. It transforms the silent movie of your appearance into a story, with gestures and words. It gives meaning to the material. Indeed, it is when we find ourselves in situations outside the bounds of speech, when we are not in a position to turn our bodies into the expression of who we are, that we are able to fully grasp what it means to have a body—particularly in moments of shame, when we are reduced to being nothing but our bodies; when we stumble; when we think we are alone but are being observed; when we are not aware of something we have just said; when we're surprised by our reflection in a window as we walk down the street. All those situations when we're just a body devoid of expressivity, of intelligence.

For Jacques Derrida, it is when he is alone with his cat that he best understands what it is to have a body, the raw materiality of physical appearance. We are at that moment face-to-face with a being that does not speak and for whom our own speech has no meaning. And without recourse to the artifice of conversation, of seduction, of social and cultural codes, we are nothing but a body, exposed, naked. "I often ask myself, just to see, *who I am*—and who I am (following) at the moment when, caught naked, in silence, by the gaze of an animal, for example the eyes of a cat, I have trouble, yes, a bad time overcoming my embarrassment. Whence this malaise? I have trouble repressing a reflex of shame . . . the single, incomparable and original experience of the impropriety that would come from appearing in truth naked, in front of the insistent gaze of the animal. . . . It is as if I were ashamed, therefore, naked in front of this cat."[4]

This radical experience gives us the unique opportunity of seeing ourselves as we are and, by the same token, of accepting ourselves. For all those who are uneasy in their own body, this confrontation with a cat's gaze is an ordeal that is both troubling and fortifying. Those who get through it will gain in self-confidence and be more comfortable meeting the gaze of other human animals.

THE LAST ACT IS TRAGIC

ENGAGING WITH PHILOSOPHY often requires us to up-end our point of view, to see the end as the true beginning. So it is that certain philosophers, such as Epicurus, Marcus Aurelius, or Montaigne, strive to demonstrate that living means nothing, that what matters is to live with the thought of death. Philosophy, from that perspective, is not so much the art of living as a meditation on death. While men may try to live as if they will never die, the philosopher seems to live every day as if it is her last.

Learning to master the terrible truth that to live is to be fated to die is the task for which philosophical therapy prepares us. But can we truly imagine our own death? And what, exactly, are we supposed to think about death? That all things pass? That we need to seize every moment? Or, on the contrary, that we must live as if we were going to live forever?

Diagnosis

"Life goes on." "Time heals all wounds." "It's better this way, his suffering is over." In practice, consolatory clichés like these can be more irritating than comforting. For death has arrived and everything has come to a halt. We even hesitate to use the term because it scares us, because it describes an unvarnished, definitive reality against which we are helpless, something obscene that offends and disgusts in equal measure. We say that he has left us, that he is gone; at a stretch we may announce that he is deceased. But dead? No. "Neither the sun nor death can be looked at without blinking," says François de La Rochefoucauld in his *Maxims*. The death we see is never our own, it's always someone else's, someone dear to us, and therefore wears the face of mourning. Death suspends everything and subverts our belief in the uninterrupted flow of days and years, the evidence of presence and connection. It is not the passage of time, the ephemeral nature of our lives, that we experience at such moments but the sense of an absolute, categorical void. It is the only moment of our entire existence as living beings when we are forced to look directly into the abyss of nothingness.

This ordeal is not suited to metaphor, which will tend to compare it to a loss or a breach. Disappointment, renunciation, and heartbreak are not the same as grief. Leaving is not dying—it's not even close. Death cannot be compared to anything else; there's no equivalent to what it puts us through. Neither death nor grief can be repaired by force of will or resilience. They do not lend themselves to literature, do not allow themselves to be turned into stories, because we are loath to use the words that serve us in life and in peace to describe them. We do not pass unscathed through the death of a loved one; we carry its burden with us forever. Death is definitively outside of life, forever unsurvivable and unbearable. It does not frighten us; it horrifies us.

We understand that death does not lie ahead but that it precedes us, that it has always been there, that it is our fate, our condition, and our destiny. Montaigne's definition of friendship—"[B]ecause it was he, because it was I"[1]—assumes its full meaning in the pain of mourning. What we were to each other, what he was to me and I was to him, dies with him forever. Even if my grief obligates me to keep him alive in memory, he is gone all the same, and the mobility of our friendship is replaced by the static solitude of the one left behind.

Placebos

So long as we are here, that means that death is somewhere else. It is on continuous delay. Strictly speaking, it has nothing to do with us; while we are alive it does not exist, and once it arrives we're gone. It's either death or us, and never the twain shall meet. "Death is nothing to us," Epicurus tells us.[2] The only thing we have to live is life itself, and life alone. It is our job, therefore, not to think about death but to profit from every moment of our life that we're able to snatch from death's grasp. We must not worry about tomorrow but enjoy today. "Seize the day, place in the hours that come as little faith as you can."[3]

This course of treatment through the present moment, or rather of the moment without tomorrows, is, however, unstable and therefore ineffective. First, because living in the present does not anesthetize our fear of the end. Who has never felt her throat tighten at the thought that her current happiness must come to an end? Time itself is nothing but death, the fact that all things must pass and never return. The present itself has almost ceased to exist by the time I experience it. The worm is in the fruit, and she who eats one must of necessity swallow the other.

Furthermore, the idea that death is nothing to us does not stand the test of grief. Even if our pain eventually grows dull, it is false and almost indecent to suggest that time heals all wounds. The death of a loved one does not occur just once; it is repeated every day. Every day, it is somehow updated. We do not miss that person today only; we miss her for all days to come. Can philosophy heal that wound? Should it even be healed? Can death be cured?

Therapy

"What always amazes me," writes Albert Camus, "when we are so swift to elaborate on other subjects, is the poverty of our ideas on death. . . . Death and colors are things we cannot discuss."[4] We clam up faced with death and mourning. "The last act is tragic, however happy all the rest of the play is," Blaise Pascal tells us. "At the last a little earth is thrown upon our head, and that is the end for ever."[5] Period. The rest is just literature and vain solace. There is a violence to life that kills the ones we love and muffles the audience's laughter.

Prescription: Diversion

We are unable to tolerate absolute sadness or the blinding light. There is no remedy for something we're not even able to look at and that can barely be endured. To live is to admit that nothing heals sorrow. Those who seek to comfort us in our pain do nothing but exacerbate it. As Montaigne suggests, we must instead favor our patients' grief "and express some approbation of their sorrow."[6]

We have to try to administer small doses of change where the grief of mourning holds exclusive sway, improvise some sort of variety in a life that seems to have come to a halt and is as if dispossessed of itself, haunted by loss. We must not console, much less encourage, but try to divert. "Variation ever relieves, dissolves, and dissipates." We don't fight pain, we use our cunning against it, "shifting place, business, and company."[7] We dissipate suffering by taking other paths, other journeys, by thinking of other things. We do not struggle against an obsessive thought or an overwhelming pain; we disperse it by surrounding it with other thoughts and other concerns.

We step aside, we turn our gaze elsewhere. The more we focus on details and trivial, superficial questions, the better chance we have of being absorbed by them and thereby distracting ourselves for a brief while from death's irruption into our life.

NOTHING IS MORE DESPICABLE
THAN ILLNESS

DEATH IS ALWAYS for some other time. The old saying "Where there's life, there's hope" perfectly illustrates the impossibility of living as if we were going to die. But death also wears the face of illness, which is a kind of death in life.

"There is nothing more despicable in this respect than illness,"[1] says Camus. It's a kind of decomposition or sapping of life. How can we live when we know that life contains the seed of its own self-destruction?

Consultation

Illness is all-consuming. You sweat, it hurts everywhere—in the bones, in the eyes, outside, inside—your limbs feel leaden; your vision is blurry; you're overtaken by chills, clammy inertia, and exhaustion that feels as if it will go on forever. Illness does not wipe us out; it takes us over body and soul. It is everywhere and nowhere; it prevents us from being ourselves, from moving, from walking, and even from thinking. We are both possessed, the host of a foreign agent, and dispossessed of ourselves; everything we normally do without giving it a second thought becomes insurmountable: getting out of bed, thinking, breathing. In that sense, good health can be thought of as the silence of our organs,[2] when our body gives us no problems, when it functions without our help, without our needing to worry about it. A healthy body is one that is not organic but mechanical, a beautiful machine that doesn't even need to be rewound, that runs by itself like a clock, without a hitch, with no sand in its gears. Furthermore, illness is not something that happens to the body alone; it afflicts every part of us: our personality, our character, our will. This is not incidental; it's a way of life that we are compelled to adopt, especially when the illness is chronic and reminds us of its presence every day—a disease that does not kill but that is also never cured.

Like a cuckoo or a parasite, it sets up shop wherever there is life, it circulates through our veins, it colonizes the air in our lungs and the ideas in our mind. It is life itself that has grown sick, not so much contaminated by death but emptied of its substance: a life without life, that is the ordeal of illness. The body that was ours, integral to what we were, is now an alien body, pored over, auscultated, perfused, divided into regions that we are unable even to name. Illness delivers us to the duality of medicine that distinguishes the mind from the body in order to build a case, a series of symptoms, a cascade of technical and organic breakdowns. It is not Descartes who inflicted the duality of soul and body on our culture—it's the doctors.

Therapeutic Failures

You have to fight, keep yourself going, stiffen your upper lip. The patient has to be a soldier: defeat is unthinkable and resistance mandatory. You have to struggle against the enemy disease within.

This is a trial, and like all trials it has its winners and its losers. The patient must be a fighter. We may even be tempted to envy her, since illness offers her the chance to surpass herself, to put her resources and strength to the test. Don't they say that what doesn't kill us makes us stronger? The patient has the opportunity to be a hero, to plant her flag at the summit of fever, the peak of cancer. Why not sing the national anthem and wave to the crowd while you're at it?

Nothing is more revolting than this moralization of disease, which necessarily blames the patient for her own illness. While keeping your spirit up is essential, healing is not an athletic competition and being sick is not the consequence of a lack of training or the outcome of laziness. The patient is no more forced to fight than she is responsible for her illness; we don't create our own cancer any more than we are compelled to vanquish it in single combat. Continuing to live against all odds is already more than sufficient. Such warlike similes aim at giving meaning where there is none, at finding reasons, sources, causes, goals, and scores where there is nothing but the unjustified misrule of disease. How can we consent to burdening the patient's suffering with the anguish of blame? Is the patient who fails to recover a loser?

Behind these exhortations to fight illness are some very indecent and dangerous notions, such as those of weakness, defeat, and even cowardice. Is it that our concept of health is based on the idea of sports, demanding that we remain infallibly in shape? Or is it a way of importing the demands of the working world—the need for results, productivity, pride, self-actualization—into the realm of health? Illness is not a war because it has nothing to do with creating heroes. The best we can hope for is to live with it, and that in itself is quite enough.

Philosophical Cure

Illness, as we've said, is not incidental but essential; it does not involve just one part of ourselves—body, organ, or brain—but touches on our very essence, our being. "We recover from an accidental stupor; but how is it possible to recover from complete exhaustion? . . . That is really what is most sad in those slow diseases . . . we feel existence undermined in its very depth; it is that we feel like a tree seeing its very roots torn to pieces—like a mountain assisting at its own overthrow. . . . Annihilation—or, at least dispersion, dissolution"[3]—that, according to the nineteenth-century French philosopher Jean-Marie Guyau, is the truth revealed by illness. It may even be that health is not the opposite of illness but the capacity to overcome it, to use it as the basis and rationale for establishing new vital norms, new ways of keeping life alive. By that definition, health would simply be illness conquered. But how do we maintain that confidence in the vitality of life—an almost biological confidence—when we have known illness and our life has been reduced, lessened, and abused by it?

There have been philosophers, such as Descartes or Ivan Illich in the 1970s, who have suffered extreme ill health yet refused medical treatment as a way of preserving their health. If they are to be believed, those who accept medicalization have already given up on the idea of recovery. In his final hours, Descartes refused to be bled by doctors trying to save him from the pneumonia he had contracted in the service of Queen Christina of Sweden, who required him to rise at dawn, in the cold and the ice, to deliver her private philosophy lessons. "Gentlemen," he exclaimed, "spare a Frenchman's blood!" and asked instead to be given tobacco dissolved in warm wine. The body knows what it needs better than the doctor does. We must heed this organic language, which our soul registers and translates in order to teach us what is harmful and what is beneficial. A human being is not pure mind; she is the union of a soul and a body, and what affects one is felt by the other, and vice versa. Far from having banished the body from philosophy and from having promoted the divorce of the physical from the psychic, Descartes was the inventor of the psychosomatic.

According to Ivan Illich, "The medical establishment has become a major threat to health"[4] because it strips the patient of the characteristics of the living. The medical system expropriates health, or rather the patient, who is denied all decision-making power over herself and her body. While such rejections of medicine may be radical and do not offer a cure for leukemia or infectious rheumatism, they nevertheless testify to the patient's need to retain control over her own body and mind, her actions and her decisions, whereas disease and the medical world tend in the other direction, toward depersonalization and objectification.

A Patient's Rights: Illness Is Not a Metaphor

According to Aristotle, some metaphors can be inappropriate.[5] Making a metaphor of illness by speaking of it as a battle to be waged is inappropriate. Falling ill cannot be compared to a failure, to a battle that may have been lost but won't stop you from winning the war. This graphic and moralizing lexicon ("You can't give up," "You have to fight it") represents both ignorance of what disease really is and an exercise in blaming the patient. If there's any battle to be waged here, it's the one to prohibit any attempt (martial or moral) to make a metaphor of illness. For, as the American philosopher Susan Sontag maintains with regard to cancer, "illness is not a metaphor, and . . . the most truthful way of regarding illness—and the healthiest way of being ill—is to resist such metaphoric thinking."[6]

The contamination begins when we stop calling illness by its name, when we start seeing it as something other than what it is, the result of anxiety, an opportunity to embrace life more tightly, to hang on to it, to fight, to learn to be vulnerable. Any speech that conceals the violent, brutal, and abhorrent reality of illness should be proscribed. Even if the mental aspect is critical and has a role to play in maintaining the body's health, even if the psychosomatic aspect is real, that must not lead us to attribute any didactic power to illness. It has no lesson to teach; it doesn't even have a meaning.

It is the doorway into another life, "the night-side of life, a more onerous citizenship. Everyone who is born holds dual citizenship, in the kingdom of the well and in the kingdom of the sick. Although we all prefer to use only the good passport, sooner or later each of us is obliged, at least for a spell, to identify ourselves as citizens of that other place."[7]

SUFFERING

PAIN IS WHAT tells me I have a body, that I'm alive, and that I can't take being alive for granted, that life can falter. We can't ignore suffering, yet we are barely able to verbalize it. At best it is able to draw a shriek out of us, and of course the fearful awareness that existence can be cruel and violent. Through this dire revelation, we understand that to be alive is to be susceptible to feeling pain.

We may all be familiar with Descartes's famous *cogito ergo sum,* but how many of us know that the *Meditations* contains another foundational experience of the self—one that is mediated by suffering. Through pain, I am fully my own body. Unable to put any distance at all between myself and what it feels, I am indeed nothing but my own body, as the pain it endures negates everything that is not it: "Nor was it without some reason that I believed that this body (which by a certain special right I call my own) belonged to me more properly and more strictly than any other; for in fact I could never be separated from it as from other bodies; I experienced in it and on account of it all my appetites and affections."[1]

Clinical Profile

Faced with pain, we can only cry out, weep, and endure. Our very being feels entirely absorbed and invaded by it; the air grows thin, the world recedes, and time is reduced to the present moment. We have become nothing but an open wound, without past or future, without memory or history, without the strength to speak or desire. It's as if everything we are has been swept away and suspended by suffering. We are no more than the expression of pain, as if we no longer had an interior life, a place to withdraw to, where we are safe to remain ourselves or, at least, to be anything other than the pain that has overwhelmed us.

Strictly speaking, we no longer exist, we have lost all room to maneuver—we are nothing but suffering. We can't even understand what we are going through, we can barely describe it. Not one part of us is spared. We are not in pain here or there but everywhere. We have to strain just to avoid disappearing, evaporating, being disarticulated by the pain, be it physical or emotional. Does such an experience really give us anything worth thinking about?

Remedy

Popular wisdom agrees with Greek tragedy in affirming that we learn through suffering. But what exactly is it that we learn? What lesson can suffering have to teach us? Does it even have a meaning, and thus a value, a life lesson to impart? Some people insist that we can metabolize suffering, that is, convert its negative energy into positive, do something with it. As if there were some sort of profundity about pain, a truth to be discovered, from which we might emerge stronger, more dignified, and more mature.

That is the twofold danger of the cult of suffering, which sanctifies pain by turning it into an opportunity to achieve dignity and moral stature, and that sees pain as an apprenticeship and a source of knowledge. But that would be to undermine the "solidarity of the shaken" described by the Czech philosopher Jan Patočka, that "solidarity of those who are capable of understanding what life and death are all about, and so what history is about."[2] Those who have endured suffering know that there's nothing to be done with it. You live apart; you try to exist despite it, around it, wherever it leaves you a scrap of room and respite. You can't metabolize suffering; you can't transform it, either into fuel to propel you on your way or into the material for creation, writing, or drawing. Suffering is a stone: it has neither blood nor flesh, neither meaning nor purpose. The only thing we are able to do is to listen to the lamentations of those who suffer.

The Ricoeur Method, or Complaint Therapy

We should neither banalize suffering, by seeing it as an accident to be overcome, nor magnify it, by giving it the power to reveal something about our being or our personality. Suffering is always outrageous; we are not improved or strengthened by the ordeal. "To suffer is to suffer too much," Paul Ricoeur affirms. Philosophy has a certain utility in this respect that some people may think paradoxical—it rejects anything that seeks to make a positive out of the negative side of this painful experience. You don't narrate suffering, you endure it. Nor do you delegate it; I am the one suffering, no one else. Suffering separates me from others; it "excommunicates" me by divesting me of initiative, movement, even willpower, and condemning me to passivity.

True, the worst pain makes the best poems and the fiercest philosophers, but creation only comes later, once the stunning shock of suffering has abated. So long as it persists, no daylight can penetrate the shadow it casts.

Through complaint, however, I regain a certain kind of autonomy, status, life. If suffering is the exact opposite of action—the experience of radical impotence—complaint is a gesture toward action at the very core of that impotence, a drive to evade my excommunication and exile. We're not talking here about whiners or hypochondriacs, people afraid of their own shadows, the fainthearted who are undone by any little setback and are perfectly comfortable in the role of victim. This is about the terse and sober complaint that denounces the violence of existence, that is both "recrimination" and "indictment": Why me? How long? Why now?

The only philosophy really worth its salt is that which respects complaint, and hence suffering, and rejects optimistic encouragement. "Whatever the solution to these enigmas may be, one frame of mind is unacceptable—that is, optimism, which someone once defined as the caricature of a hope that has never shed a tear."[3]

AGING

AGING IS A little like a death that happens every day, but insidiously, without fanfare or pain, without our really being aware of it, until one fine day we wake up old, tired, and spent. It's only once it has fled that we understand the extent to which youth was more than just a phase of life, more than just a matter of age. It's a unique way of life, without equivalent or substitute, that will never return. As the sixteenth-century poet Pierre de Ronsard told it, "Man's true wealth is green youth. The rest of our years are but winters."[1]

To be young is to enjoy that combination of levity and enthusiasm, the somewhat flippant and addled attitude of someone who has time ahead of him. It is to live without counting, without addition or subtraction, without regrets or timid hopes. How do we recover from the loss of youth? "Farewell, pleasant sun . . . My body is descending to the place where everything falls apart." Old age flays us of our skin and our flesh: "All I have left is bones, I am like a skeleton, un-fleshed, un-nerved, un-muscled, un-pulped."[2]

Radiology

Simone de Beauvoir wrote: "I often stop, flabbergasted, at the sight of this incredible thing that serves me as my face. . . . Perhaps the people I pass in the street see merely a woman in her fifties who simply looks her age, no more, no less. But when I look, I see a face as it was, attacked by the pox of time for which there is no cure."[3] A pox that disfigures me without destroying me altogether. It's still my face, same features, recognizable, the eyes and the expressions, too, for sure, but I am not what I see. I am not that face, yet it's mine. Deep down, in my mind, I'm still twenty and I don't look like that. More than at any other time in our lives, in old age we feel the difference between inside and outside, between what we think we are and what we appear to be.

Aging is a metamorphosis, probably the only one given to us in this life. I am still the same even as I change. Strictly speaking, I—the I that is me—have not aged, and yet in my body as in my mind, in my thoughts as in my gestures, in my desires, and my pleasures I feel an irremediable loss that I will never recoup. Not only a loss of memory and nimbleness—of character and movement—but also a loss of momentum and color. My world, my life, my being are washing out.

We stop moving forward in any meaningful way, we slow down. In any case, for that matter, we're not going anywhere anymore, we've reached our destination. "Old age fills [us] with more aversion than death itself. And indeed, it is old age, rather than death, that is to be contrasted with life. Old age is life's parody. . . . There is only one solution if old age is not to be an absurd parody of our former life, and that is to go on pursuing ends that give our existence meaning—devotion to individuals, to groups or to causes, social, political, intellectual or creative work."[4] We must learn how to keep our desires, anger, and lusts alive so we are not trampled or frittered to death.

Remedy

But growing old isn't merely a matter of age; it's a problem of inertia. We grow old when we settle for carrying on, rather than initiating new beginnings. We long ago abandoned any effort to perpetuate the illusion that we are all able to reinvent ourselves, that if you want to change, you need only decide to do so, and that every option and every possibility remains on the table. That would be confusing art with life, imagining ourselves the impresarios of our own lives, making and unmaking at whim; it is the belief that willing is the same as creating, even though the conditions surrounding our choices have been imposed on us and "we have been cast into the world without first being consulted."[5] The mere fact of having been born at a particular moment, in a particular place, with a particular face and personality, is an a priori constraint on our so-called power of self-invention. To live is to accept facts about our circumstances that we have not decided for ourselves.

But in our private space, where our will can dictate its own freedom and test its room for maneuver, we can "actively be what we are by chance."[6] We can test the limits of our birthright, exercise our capacity to launch new projects, without disruption or heroics, but modestly, by cultivating our own power of new beginnings. That's because what we are by birth is not solely a biological phenomenon, any more than old age or youth; it is, according to Hannah Arendt, the power to create new realities, howsoever uncertain or frail.[7] It is to harbor the impulse to initiate. It's not about spreading yourself thin with constant activity but about struggling resolutely and calmly against the weight of things and all that is inexorable and unchanging in the world. It is to make things happen—again, humbly but with unpredictable, surprising results. It is to act the way we confess, by shining a light on an unseen, unexpected reality.

The Natality Cure

It is inevitable that youth is lost, that summer fades, and that life ends. By its very nature time is fleeting and passes, never to return. There are no second chances; that is the cruel truth revealed by aging through the implacable reality of time's irreversibility. We cannot come and go as we please through time, and nothing lasts forever. Life marches forward toward old age and away from all that will never return and that cannot be undone once accomplished.

And yet there is a way to reverse that deadly slope and reascend it. As Hannah Arendt tells us, it is to inaugurate new beginnings, to bring something new into the world, to enrich reality with choices and initiatives, and thereby to promote natality over inertia. Both action and speech give us the ability to "dispose of the future as though it were the present," to plunge in, to innovate, to forestall time, to catch the future unawares. It's "the enormous and truly miraculous enlargement" of the dimension in which we normally live our lives.

We are more than mere birds of passage, without constancy or a hold on the passage of time, "doomed to swing forever in the ever-recurring cycle of becoming." Nor are we under house arrest, reduced to living exclusively in the present, groaning under the weight of constraints and predetermined circumstance. We have the capacity to interrupt the "inexorable automatic course of daily life," to give the lie to the law that says that "[i]f left to themselves, human affairs can only follow the law of mortality."

While nothing lasts and nothing is ever certain, it is nevertheless true that through our actions and the words we speak we can delay fate and sabotage destiny, reminding ourselves "that men, though they must die, are not born in order to die but in order to begin."[8]

TOBACCO, ALCOHOL, AND ADDICTION

PASSION, OBSESSION, AMBITION, addiction—everything that excites or torments us—represents one of the great fields of application for the philosophy cure. Whatever it is that ails you, it all comes down to your passions. And it is philosophy, far more than psychiatry, that has drawn up the most accurate clinical profile of those passions. The most enduring, too. Jean Esquirol, a father of French psychiatry in the nineteenth century, reprised the teaching of the first-century Stoics to develop his theory of madness and mental illness.[1]

Chrysippus, one of the earliest Stoic masters, believed that there were several basic forms of madness, some of which included: madness for wine (*oinophlugia*), madness for women (*gynaikomania*), and madness for fame (*doxomania*). Because they cannot be satiated, such desires are irrational and drive men mad, turning them into disconsolate slaves.

All are addictions: irrepressible needs that take possession of us without bringing any real joy or pleasure.

Symptoms

Love takes root in the stomach. Your stomach and guts feel as if they were white-hot—he's looking at me, she's talking to me, he's going to call me, she loves me, I love him. Your heart panics; an electric current courses through your body, painful and sensual at the same time. He loves me, I love him. Romantic passion borrows from every medical condition; it's fever, color blindness, and tachycardia all in one. It can make you shiver or sweat for no reason; it modifies colors and perceptions. It's a disorder of the temperament that pointlessly amplifies every emotion, and a mental alienation that irreparably distorts your relationship to reality.

Our capacity to discriminate is upended. The trivial becomes essential, the marginal vital, the immediate is all that matters, and facts are falsified wholesale. This explains both the absurdity and the obstinacy of the lover—he magnifies the little things and behaves with such intensity that you can't help admiring him even as you laugh at him. It's as if he were running on a different voltage. It's as if he's been electrified, more nerves than flesh, irradiated. His condition verges on madness.

While seventeenth-century treatises cited an endless list of passions, the only one we are capable of grasping nowadays is love, as if it were the root of all passions, their common denominator. Ambition, jealousy, sadness, fear, and joy become mere facets of love. Passion is in effect a fixation of desire and willpower on one object. But the aim isn't even of being happy—it's of loving. "'Well! Contemplate Phaedra then in all her fury. I love,'"[2] says Racine's great tragic heroine. In our passion, we do not love someone in particular; we merely love. Love spills forth without limit, without any real object. Or rather, the object—a man, a woman—is merely the occasion, the trigger, which love immediately and overwhelmingly subsumes, as if it were only waiting for a pretext to run amok. This can be a blinding experience, since the lover is interested in loving and not in the beloved. That is why, after passion ebbs, we may come to our senses, wondering how we ever found ourselves in such a state.

We are often overinvested in our passion, and with a dispro-portionate sense of urgency, as if it were a question of life and death, when it really comes down to nothing more than a roll of the dice, or a relationship of which we will recall surprisingly little once the passion has withered. But, as certain neuroscience studies have shown, it also explains why passion and strong emotions can facilitate decision-making by providing the momentum, the total commitment, that extinguishes apathy and vacillation once and for all.[3]

Passion is all about paradox. It makes you want to die for some-one whom you'll end up caring nothing for. It makes you feel fully alive and at the same time totally out of control. You are convinced that yours is a unique experience that overrides all ordinary rules, and yet you describe and nurture your love with words written by other people, scenes from the movies, and repartee torn from nov-els. You are no longer master of yourself and yet you're capable of making the most sophisticated calculations; you think of yourself as genuine, sincere, authentic, and yet you constantly dissimulate, pretend, and simper. These are the paradoxes of intensity, which is both excessive and superficial, boundless and miserly, grandil-oquent and inattentive. It's a combustion—a flame that burns but does not heat, a fire that does not consume—a story without a fu-ture, even when it lasts for years.

Therapeutic Failure

What is unhealthy about passion is not the passion itself but its ex-cessiveness. It causes damage only when it is immoderate, greedy, impatient, obsessive, and paranoid. When passion is stripped of hyperbole, it becomes strength of character, driving impulse, re-solve, life force. According to Aristotle, it may even be a virtue, "an intermediate between excess and defect."[4] In the same way, courage is the intermediate between the two opposing passions of cowardice and recklessness; temperance, the happy median between apathy and profligacy. Even anger may be a virtue that is aroused by righteousness, at an equal distance between spinelessness, which cowers in fear, and aggression, which finds offense in everything. So we can make passion reasonable, ensure that it remains pleasurable, and does not spill over into an addiction that afflicts and enslaves us and is ultimately a cause of suffering.

But it's not the happy medium we seek; it's excess. It is not satiation but hunger; it is not satisfaction but profusion. To be impassioned is to want to live beyond our needs, to want *more* and *again*. As Shakespeare's King Lear puts it, "'Allow not nature more than nature needs / Man's life is cheap as beast's.'"[5] It's that "more" that makes us feel alive, that turns our life into a yarn to spin, since what is our life story made of if not passions, of loves thwarted or shared? Aristotle's clinical error is to believe that it's a problem of degree, that if you dial down their intensity, the passions can be tamed. But a passion is not an affinity that morphs into obsession or a partiality that becomes an addiction. A passion does not become immoderate; it is immoderate by its very nature. And if it can be contained, disciplined, or limited, it's only because it was never a passion but a mere fancy. Anger that can be tempered is not anger; it is innately "unbridled and unmanageable,"[6] as the Stoic philosopher Seneca rightly observes.

Philosophical Therapy

Passion is not emotion but servitude. You do not dominate a passion; it dominates you. "A passion . . . consists not in being affected by the sights which are presented to us, but in giving way to our feelings and following up these chance promptings,"[7] Seneca continues. An impassioned man will never be at peace; he will be tortured, insatiable, forever unsatisfied. What he wants is not to possess the object of his desire but to make it disappear. The miser wants money not to use as a medium of exchange but to bury and thus negate its function. The ambitious man wants power so as to later eliminate and deprive others of it. The lover does not want the beloved alive and thus potentially unfaithful; he wants her dead. The perfect representation of passion is Cranach's painting of Salome, clad in purple and gold, holding the head of John the Baptist on a platter.

The answer to passion's deadly power cannot be the happy medium. It lies, on the contrary, in total eradication. That is the medicine offered by Stoicism. It must be radical because the passions do not permit half measures—impossible to contain by their very nature, they call for uncompromising treatment. That which cannot be controlled must be rejected. But what we lose in passion we gain in willpower. We do not forbid pleasure by banning addiction; we rediscover it. "You may do the same things fearlessly and with greater accuracy of judgment, and . . . feel even the pleasures more than before."[8]

Treatment by Ataraxia

The Stoical cure consists of never beginning, because it is easier not to feel passion than to stop feeling it. Passion is always stronger than we are; to consent to it is to lose ourselves to it. Thus, rather than fool ourselves that it can make us happy and that we can curb its excesses, it is better never to succumb to it. "Let us therefore resist these faults when they are demanding entrance, because, as

I have said, it is easier to deny them admittance than to make them depart." Such is Seneca's radical cure. "Knowing our weakness, let us remain quiet." The name of that quiet is ataraxia—the peace that rules the soul when it has made itself a fortress.

Contrarily, the impassioned man is someone who is bound to anxiety because the object of his adoration can be taken from him, and with it his very raison d'être. What will I do without my iPhone, my children, my money, my lover? Passions are delirious convictions that we mistake for reality; for the passionate, as for the superstitious and the paranoid, the world is crawling with clues that are cause for hope or fear. He asked me if I take sugar with my coffee—does that mean he loves me? She smiled at him; she must be cheating on me. And so on.

The Stoics—a school of thinkers who taught from fourth-century BCE Greece through the reign of the Roman emperor Marcus Aurelius in the second century CE—have traditionally been reproached for the inhuman and disagreeable nature of their morality. It is not only impossible but scarcely desirable to live without passions. That would be to live like a stone, without innards or flesh. To which Seneca replies that it is our devotion to the passions and the ignorance in which they plunge us that makes us "prefer to make excuses for them rather than shake them off."[9] The impassioned man who insists that they are stronger than he is and that he cannot resist them is lying to himself. It is not that he cannot fight off his passions; it's that he doesn't want to.

"If you want something badly enough, you can have it." That is the only possible treatment for passion, directly inspired by the Stoic principle that "Where there's a will, there's a way."

The Dietetics of Pleasure

ONE AFFIRMATION OF common sense that should require no sophisticated philosophy to be recognized as obvious is that you must seek pleasure and flee pain. No one can be happy without pleasure. Science confirms the ineluctable logic that pleasure is the motor force of the brain. It is through the impetus of pleasure that the brain sorts through the information and signals coming both from within the body and from the outside world so as to adapt our conduct to our environment and ensure our survival and autonomy. Pleasure, therefore, is in no way a mere concept; it is the very foundation of how we, so-called rational animals, conduct our lives.

How does this component of our being, more physiological than psychological, become a philosophical problem? And by what twist of logic have we managed to turn pleasure into an offense and to inject complexity into what is innocently and simply pleasurable?

Consultation

Long summer nights, intimate conversation among friends, a lover's touch, rising laughter, the writings of Hegel or Rimbaud, reunions, a long-awaited answer . . . We feel pleasure and everything within and around us seems to fall silent. There is a kind of lull, something lovely and buoyant that wafts calmly on the breeze. Like pain, pleasure makes disengagement impossible and is wholly absorbing. We are submerged and lose ourselves in our feelings. Onomatopoeia best describes such gratification, just as screaming best expresses suffering. There is total surrender in pleasure, a kind of return to a preverbal state in which the body and the mind commune in shared rapture. Pleasure is like a vise that has been loosened, a tension that has been relaxed, allowing us to see the truth about how we live the rest of our lives in the absence of pleasure, in anxiety and gloom. We sigh with pleasure because we feel both absolved of pain and relieved of a burden.

Pleasure is like an unexpected bonus, a gift that we have neither earned nor prepared for, since prearranged pleasures are always the most disappointing. Pleasure is delectation and delight, whereas desire is movement: it whirls, grinds, marches on, rambles. Desire is hardworking and industrious; pleasure is lazy and contemplative. Desire does not end with satisfaction but is revived by it—unlike need, which like hunger, thirst, and sexual attraction vanishes once fulfilled. Desire seeks desire, so much so that for every desire we satisfy ten more arise to take its place: "No achieved object of willing gives lasting, unwavering satisfaction; rather, it is only ever like the alms thrown to a beggar that spares his life today so that his agony can be prolonged until tomorrow,"[1] Schopenhauer tell us.

The disease of desire is therefore a kind of greed that can never get enough and whose political avatar is the tyrant, described by Montaigne's dear friend Étienne de La Boétie as the "inhuman . . . savage beast . . . man-eater" that enslaves and devours.[2] The disease of pleasure is one not of voracious insatiability but of lists. Unlike desire, it does not seek *more* but *many*—first do this, then that, then the other. Pleasure is a collector. Where is the harm in that? How could it cause suffering?

Therapeutic Failure: The Callicles Method, or the Sorrow of the Colander

Surely the harm lies in the very opposite—in no longer feeling pleasure, in being satiated? That would be like "the life of a stone," Callicles tells Socrates, in the only dialogue written by Plato in which philosophy appears to lose the argument. "No, in good truth, Socrates—which you claim to be seeking—the fact is this . . . [a man's life is] having all the other desires, and being able to satisfy them, and so with these enjoyments leading a happy life." Callicles's cure is that of gratification. "No, in good truth, Socrates—which you claim to be seeking—the fact is this . . . [a man's life is] having all the other desires, and being able to satisfy them, and so with these enjoyments leading a happy life."[3]

We need to understand that this is not the theory of some party boy but the principle of an aristocrat who insists on living a life worthy of his pleasures, whereas most people are happy to enjoy them in the gutter. It takes courage, not complacency, to savor our pleasures. Pleasure is the opposite of debauchery. Socrates's response is equally radical—regardless of the pretty picture Callicles tries to paint, a life of pleasure does not gratify but induces emptiness and ignorance; it's like "a vessel full of holes, because it can never be satisfied."

Our banquets, our cocktails, our dinner parties, and our nights on the town roll on and accumulate without filling either our souls or our stomachs. The sense of living in a never-ending carnival with which we try to sustain our days fuels the anxiety that we're not living a worthy life and ends in the pathetic monotony of a balance sheet. Writes Schopenhauer: "There is no more mistaken path to happiness than worldliness, revelry, high life: for the whole object of it is to transform our miserable existence into a succession of joys, delights and pleasures—a process which cannot fail to result in disappointment and delusion; on a par, in this respect, with its obligato accompaniment, the interchange of lies."[4] There's something burdensome about our frenzy of activity that makes it more like work, like labor performed without pleasure. It's no coincidence that we say we're "doing" Burning Man or an exhibition at the Smithsonian, as if they were a series of tasks. By piling one amusement onto the next we deprive them of the buoyancy and superficiality that are what makes them so pleasurable in the first place.

Recommendation

For all that, philosophy does not advocate abstinence or asceticism—with the exception of Epicurus, who, contrary to common belief, is capable of whipping up a philosopher's banquet out of bread and water. The Epicurean doctrine aside, philosophy is not an abstract cuisine without aroma or flavor, if only because abstraction itself is a pleasure, and practicing philosophy is a source of both intellectual and sensual delight. We must cultivate not that which debilitates and disheartens but that which fortifies. Tears and laments do not get us any deeper into the heart of the matter but are expressions of our powerlessness, the effect of all that diminishes us. Spinoza writes: "Therefore, to make use of what comes in our way, and to enjoy it as much as possible (not to the point of satiety, for that would not be enjoyment) is the part of a wise man."[5]

Note how Spinoza takes care in his recommendation to stress moderation, given that pleasures are always made of flammable material. And even when they are moderate, they are always condemned to being on the list, the inert modality of bookkeeping. How do we get around that? Camus, following up on Nietzsche, suggests the Mediterranean Thought cure.

The So-called Mediterranean Thought Cure

The Mediterranean Sea as cure—no surprise there. The sun, the sea, the wind, the remote and arid splendor of the southern landscape sing of the love affair not only between man and nature but between man and life. That, according to Camus, is "Mediterranean thought," a doctrine that finds happiness in our reconciliation with existence, despite all that may be bitter or disappointing about it.

The pleasure felt in this way is neither frenzied nor hyperactive. It is instead akin to the noble refusal to be satisfied with what we have: "How many hours have I spent . . . trying to match my breathing with the world's tumultuous sighs! Deep among wild scents and concerts of somnolent insects, I open my eyes and heart to the unbearable grandeur of this heat-soaked sky. It is not so easy to become what one is, to rediscover one's deepest measure."[6]

"Rediscovering your deepest measure." This has nothing to do with serenity or self-actualization. Nor is it about endless distractions, antidotes for boredom, or even optimism. It's something more demanding that insists that we bring the full force of character to bear on the simple act of living, the strength of one who "through the virtue of its purity and its sap, stands up to all the winds that blow in from the sea. Such is the strength of character that in the winter of the world will prepare the fruit."[7]

This courage, this spirit of conquest that we bring to life provides the greatest of delights and makes of us the bold members of an aristocracy of pleasure: "I've always felt as if I lived on the high seas, threatened, at the heart of a royal happiness."[8]

AFFLICTIONS OF THE BRAIN

MIND OR BRAIN? Which one contracts illness? Which one needs curing? Where is the seat of intelligence? Where does stupidity lurk? Must philosophy lay down its weapons and scalpels in deference to more competent disciplines—the neurosciences, psychiatry, the cognitive sciences—practices that are interested not in the phantom mind but only in the very real organ we call the brain?

Case Study

The big problem with stupidity is that it thinks. There is only one *cogito* for the worthy and for the idiots alike. But while people may be able to rectify their errors, stupidity itself stands firm. It is always satisfied with itself. According to the American writer Avital Ronell, "Stupidity can be situated in terms of its own satiety, as the experience of being full, fulfilled, accomplished . . . Replete in itself, immune to criticism, without resistance or the effort of negativity, stupidity contains a sacred element: it is beatitude."[1] Nothing surprises or unsettles stupidity; it doesn't believe, it *knows*. But stupidity can also assume a more vibrant form, when it imagines everything in terms of highly wrought emotion and violins, and truth as ever restless and moving. That is when sentiment takes the place of thought. Stupidity loves virtuosity, action, and expertise, anything evincing a proactive mentality that is a stranger to doubt and nuance.

Treating stupidity is philosophy's greatest task. In reeducating thought, it seeks to restore intellectual private property. Most of the time, we do not think for ourselves but through other people, drawing from the well of dominant or militant opinion, which we express with an exotic lexicon replete with such improbable terms as "impact," "unpack," "prioritize," "debrief," "experience," "experiential." The only way to push back against such professionalized pabulum is to cultivate curiosity, which consists of rejecting mental automatism and favoring whatever we find provocative.

Dissecting, analyzing, looking under every stone—anything that diverts us from our overweening attraction to ready-made answers—is a healthy activity. Intelligence cannot be reduced to "exchanges," debates, and affirmations. It is fundamentally associated with risk-taking, anxiety, a refusal to generalize and approximate. We suffer more from imprecision than from misinformation.

Treatment

It's common knowledge that philosophy was born in prison. "Behold! human beings living in an underground den." All they see are shadows, which they take for reality. That is how Plato's famous allegory of the cave, or the prison of ignorance, begins. "And if he is compelled to look straight at the light, will he not have a pain in his eyes which will make him turn away to take refuge in the objects of vision which he can see, and which he will conceive to be in reality clearer than the things which are now being shown to him?"[2] What a comfort it is to have a (personal) opinion always at hand and in mind. For it is not nature that abhors a vacuum but education—we absolutely have to prove that we know, that we have something to say, that we have a ready answer. It is indeed easier and faster to snatch at the views wafting by on the breeze of conventional wisdom than to think for oneself, starting from scratch and without preconceived ideas or ready-made opinions.

That's why philosophy is such a painful and unpleasant form of therapy, whatever those who would present it as the love child of yoga and Miss Lonelyhearts may say. Philosophy is neither the art of conversation nor an exercise in shared emotions—it is a concept factory.[3] And a concept is always the fruit of an ascetic impulse, an exercise in self-denial by which we disrupt our natural and spontaneous tendency to hold an opinion about everything. While a concept may help us to learn something, it does so only if we push back against our immoderate attraction to the known, to everything we have always thought and believed. We must confront the unknown and resist looking for a familiar face, seeing only what we want to see, hearing only the songs that everyone else is singing. Thinking means forcing yourself, agreeing to see things as they are without automatically stamping them with your own judgments and beliefs.

But we are incorrigible tourists. By land and by sea, in our thoughts as in our conversations, we always seek to bring everything back around to what we know. We rack up one comparison after another and use our reading lists to avoid feeling homesick and map out every novelty. We find that Bali is a little like Key West, that happiness is like a child's smile, that democracy means doing whatever we want, that truth is purely subjective, and so on. And just to make absolutely sure that we have immured the unknown within the known, we rush to take pictures of everything even before looking at it, transforming things and ideas into snapshots.

In order to undermine that deplorable tendency, philosophy must undertake to decolonize, to free thought from all the ready-made opinions that trammel it. Anyone who wants to escape from prison or a cave must be ready to jettison all her ballast and to fly without a net if she hopes to think for herself and travel without a guide.

Descartes's "Clear and Distinct" Cure

How do we rid ourselves of our inner tourist? How do we learn to see things as they are, as if we were seeing and thinking about them for the very first time? Intelligence is young; stupidity is old—it has seen it all, heard it all, and understood it all. Thinking, on the other hand, requires us to take the time to get a handle on the unexpected, stare down the perplexing, resist the tired old responses that spontaneously come to mind. Descartes calls this intellectual discipline "meditation."

Neither Buddhist nor mindful, Descartes defines his brand of meditation as follows: "[T]o accept nothing as true which I did not clearly recognize to be so: that is to say, carefully to avoid precipitation and prejudice in judgments, and to accept in them nothing more than what was presented to my mind so clearly and distinctly that I could have no occasion to doubt it."[4] Neuroscience reprises this Cartesian prescription by defining "cognitive inhibition" as an essential component of intelligence, in that it is a distancing mechanism, rejecting any response that comes "naturally" but is more often than not inappropriate. Understanding is not knowing; it is, first and foremost, resisting.

If an idea is to truly be an idea, let alone a concept, it must be absolutely precise, with nothing vague or overly general about it. The primary hallmark of intelligence is blinding, exultant, triumphant clarity. Our thoughts must have the precision of intricate clockwork, but they must also be able to produce the unexpected, to generate surprise. No one has ever thought of things in that way; no one has ever seen them from that angle. Only then do we know that we have attained to the kingdom of the concept, where we look around as if on the first morning of creation, without bias or easy explanations.

That is the Cartesian cure. Putting it into practice requires simply that we have at least one idea of our own every day, an idea that we have come up with by ourselves, by sifting, filtering, reflecting, dissecting. A nugget.

AFFLICTIONS
OF THE SOUL

THE DISTINCTION BETWEEN afflictions of the body and afflictions of the soul is an artificial one. Everything that alters the body alters the soul, and vice versa. Nothing is ever purely physical; nothing is exclusively spiritual. Even the most mindless, least sophisticated pleasure is evaluated and experienced through consciousness and thought. There is pleasure only where there is consciousness of pleasure, and that consciousness is a major factor of any gratification experienced. "[I]f you had no memory you would not recollect that you had ever been pleased," Plato reminds us. Without memory, intelligence, or thought, and despite all the pleasures you had ever enjoyed, "your life would be the life, not of a man, but of an oyster or pulmo marinus."[1]

Just as it is impossible to sort out what part of us is nature and what part nurture, it makes no sense at all to try to distinguish between that which comes from the soul and that which is felt only by the body. Merleau-Ponty puts it this way: "It is impossible to superimpose upon man both a primary layer of behaviors that could be called 'natural' and a constructed cultural or spiritual world. For man, everything is constructed and everything is natural, in the sense that there is no single word or behavior that does not owe something to mere biological being—and, at the same time, there is no word or behavior that does not break free from animal life."[2]

Pleasures are never only like those experienced by an oyster or else totally constructed; like pain, they always belong both to the soul and to the body.

But there are afflictions that more specifically target the soul, even if their symptoms are experienced directly by the body. What ailments afflict the soul? In the main, they are pathologies that threaten its freedom. Good luck, bad luck, destiny, fate, circumstance, fortune, chance—our free will is threatened from all sides, prevented from acting by timelines and events over which it has no control, or control only after the fact. Philosophy therefore offers a means of survival, both for enduring, rejecting, or avoiding misfortune, and for preserving, attracting, or enjoying good fortune.

Our free will itself is a serf will, an indentured freedom that we must manumit. What does philosophy have to offer that is both a source of healing and a principle of liberation?

LIVING

WE USUALLY ATTACH a qualifying adjective to life, as if it lacked its own intrinsic quality and content: personal life, professional life, double life, inner life. . . . Life can't be boiled down to the various nervous, cerebral, digestive, or neurovegetative systems that sustain it. It is a task that we must accomplish, and we must make something of our life if we want in turn to be someone.

We cannot help having a religious relationship with existence, viewing events and setbacks as the signs of providence and choice (be it advantageous or harmful), as if existence served a goal and obeyed some logic. That would seem to suggest that life itself is not enough for us; it must also have a meaning and a truth that orders and guides it.

Consultation

"I am, I exist," affirms the great Descartes, with all the elation that only the most baffling metaphysical truths can elicit. But what life am I living for? True, it takes a failure, something on which to stumble and fall, to make us ask the question. We generally find a way of carrying on. Life is essentially a matter of DIY, of making do with whatever's at hand, cobbling it together at the spur of the moment, with little or no advance planning, in accordance with a system that has much in common with recycling.[1] In a certain way, our lives have gotten out ahead of us; they have already begun; we are "on our way," and the time for choosing will come later.[2] Is there at the very least some way to learn—to learn how to live the way we learn a foreign language or how to ski? What do we do with our lives? Do we fill them up by launching careers and accumulating jobs, status, and titles, answering the question of who we are by producing a well-ordered curriculum vitae?

Is there any real correlation between who I am and the life I am leading? Isn't there more to me than the acts I perform and the things that happen to me? My life is my own but I am not my life, for, according to Jean-Paul Sartre, "I have within me a host of untried but perfectly viable abilities, inclinations, and possibilities"[3] that life has not given me the opportunity to exercise. The potential source of infection lies there, in the impossibility of turning my life into a résumé, in the gap between what I am and how I live.

Shock Treatment

The philosophical shock treatment consists of rejecting all excuses—we are entirely responsible for the lives we lead because we are entirely free. Entirely free to be who we are or not to be. Not only do we make choices, but we choose to be ourselves. We choose to be cowardly, misunderstood, unlovable, or respected. Everything we do testifies to the fundamental choice we make about ourselves. We can expect no assistance and no rescue. The identity we acquire from our social status and the personality furnished by our character are nothing but false excuses, pretexts to avoid facing up to our freedom.

We are condemned to reinventing ourselves every minute, because at every minute we have the opportunity not to be the person we have been and not to lead the life we have been leading. Behind every action, even those that fail, there is a choice. So there can be no gap—no potential unexplored, no opportunity not taken—between what I am and how I live. I am none other than my life. The full reality of what I am is expressed in what I do.

That is the medicine offered by Sartre, for whom there is no failure that has not been sought and no adversity that has not been chosen. For whom there is no potentiality and no virtuality: only love that reveals itself is love, only the genius that creates is genius. There is no reality outside the actions we undertake. "No doubt this thought may seem harsh to someone who has not made a success of his life. But on the other hand, it helps people to understand that reality alone counts, and that dreams, expectations, and hopes only serve to define a man as a broken dream, aborted hopes, and futile expectations; in other words, they define him negatively, not positively."[4]

The Leibniz Method

While it may dismay those looking for an excuse for their disappointed ambitions, the treatment proposed by Sartre excites proactive and rebellious types, those who believe that it takes only willpower to succeed and that we are who we have decided to be. But we are never sufficiently free to make a tabula rasa of it, to behave as if nothing preexisted our freedom. For us, being free means finding our place in a world—physical, social—that is older than our freedom, that predates and in some ways conditions it. We do not create the conditions in which we exercise our freedom; we occupy a specific place in the world, whether we like it or not.

This limitation of my freedom and my choices should not prevent me from putting my stamp on every one of my days, and even hours. It is through action that I am able to make the life I have been given to live my own. That is the solution proposed by the German philosopher Gottfried Wilhelm Leibniz in order to thwart frustration—you must make time your own, make every moment of your existence alive and active.

You must not passively endure but build, and allow no moment of your day to lie fallow and unused. You must do so not by running around and jumping through hoops but by doing little with deep attention and focus: "It is possible to live a long life if we remain sensitive to even the most fleeting moments of our lives."[5] The only way you will have any chance of living a life that looks like you is to expand the life you have through the actions you undertake within it, banishing all insipidity and inertia.

DAILY LIFE

THE ONLY LIFE we have to live is our everyday life—the very same life we often spend a great deal of time trying to flee. All our parallel lives—inner, past, secret, eternal—can do nothing to alter the fact that our daily life is the only one we lead and that we are unable to escape. Even when it is steeped in tragedy or marked by genius, life is always, one way or another, daily.

It's not only that we are in thrall to time; it's also that our lives fall into the particular modality of repetition, habit, the trivial, and the routine. The daily is a chronic disease, with its relentless litany of hassles and troubles, this "rout of little ills"[1] (as Montaigne calls it) that wear us down but do not destroy us.

Psychopathology

If you want to understand the nature of daily life, you need only look at your calendar—a combination of constraints and necessities. A life like a program schedule, organized around the abscissa of hours and the ordinate of the to-do list. The register of daily life is largely that of compulsion. "That there is constraint and a kind of oppression in my life is not an illusion, then, nor a dialectical game, it is a brute fact of daily experience,"[2] wrote the nineteenth-century French philosopher Maurice Blondel. There is indeed a kind of brutality to daily life, a lack of subtlety and lightness, to the extent that those good moments that may by chance punctuate our day are always experienced both as an expansion of space and as an alleviation of our burden. Happiness is, more than anything, a measure of relief.

The brutality of constraint is compounded by the abjection of repetition—with scarce variation, it's always the same gestures, the same occupations, the same places. The effect of repetition is to blur the outlines and accentuate character to the point of caricature. The colleague who is constantly trying to get ahead ends up becoming more and more like a parody of himself, whereas our commute to the office is reduced to a handful of landmarks, two rights, three bends in the road. The everyday world is a simplified, pallid world. Almost everything about it is dispensable yet in your face. It's a world of alignments and superficiality where events occur without a storyboard or hierarchy and where the important and the insignificant carry equal weight. You would have to start from scratch, rewrite every word, to turn it into a story worthy of the name, something worth telling. Heroes have no experience of daily life; they know drama or tragedy but have never known everyday existence.

That does not mean that daily life is immune to catastrophe, but when it does arise it suspends the normal course of events—the everyday course, specifically. You can meet ordinary heroes, people like you and me who accomplish great things, but a hero in daily life is quite simply no longer a hero—it's got to be one or the other. No man is a hero to his valet, since a hero can be heroic only by turning his back on the everyday.[3] Therein lies the difference between life and narrative, reality and literature—even in the most realistic novel, there is no daily life. The mere fact of telling, plotting, and organizing it into a story suppresses the everyday.

For the life of every day is not a life in three dimensions; as we've said, everything in it is on the same level, everything in it occurs on the same and only stage. The danger, then, is to end up equating oneself with the robotic activities we engage in there, of becoming invisible. As the French novelist Raymond Queneau put it, "Ascending, descending, coming, going, a man does so much that in the end he disappears."[4]

The Bovary Placebo

We find it impossible to be satisfied living such a life and just as impossible to live any other, because every life, from the happiest to the unhappiest, must have its share of the everyday. We have only one life, but life alone will hardly suffice us. That's why we've developed an entire arsenal of additives and taste enhancers, of which literature is undoubtedly one of the most powerful. Not only because novels, poetry, tragedies, and comedies are factors of escapism and intensification in which everything is an event and everything is important—from emotions to action, including speech and sound—but also because they allow us to feel what we have never felt before, such as romantic passion, inducing that eminently literary disease known as Bovarism, which consists of having experienced the full gamut of emotions, from love to heartache, without every having really lived them.

They also offer the opportunity to relive the past, to augment our lives with a second life resurrected through the power of words. Marcel Proust describes it this way: "[T]hese resurrections of the past, for the second that they last, are so complete that . . . they force our nostrils to breathe the air of those places which are, nevertheless, so far away . . . our whole personality to believe itself surrounded by them, or at least to stumble between them and the material world. . . . So, that which the being within me, three or four times resurrected, had experienced, were perhaps fragments of lives snatched from time which, though viewed from eternity, were fugitive. And yet I felt that the happiness given me at those rare intervals in my life was the only fruitful and authentic one."[5]

Aside from the stimulants and dietary supplements provided by literature, art in general, and philosophy, we make do with our fettered days and scheduled lives. Is there any way to elude this blight, which ultimately reduces existence to a clockwork mechanism without flesh or spirit?

The Brief Habits Remedy

Tour operators, sex therapists, and psychologists encourage us to take breaks from our routine, to spice up our lives, to make an event of our experience, the way festivals around the world interrupt the ordinary course of life with their mash-ups of folkways and holiday resorts. Can life be a series of beach parties? The problem is, this kind of allegedly fun, packaged entertainment becomes just another habit that will end up boring us just as much as those it was supposed to distract us from. The solution lies in adopting brief habits, routines, and rituals that we embrace precisely in order to kick them. In this way we're able to enjoy the pleasures of settling in and escaping our comfort zones at the same time. Sedentary and nomadic, we're able to relish both predictability and change. "I love brief habits and consider them invaluable means for getting to know many things and states."

This remedy, first proposed by Nietzsche, is not about running from one activity to the next. On the contrary, it's about pausing to enjoy the comforts of enduring things and decisive choices. How wonderful it is, I could live an eternity this way—waking up early, traveling on foot, getting away from the same old people, learning to enjoy new things, drinking in new sights and sounds. . . . And then one day it's over, the brief habit has done its job. "[T]he good thing parts from me, not as something that now disgusts me but peacefully and sated with me, as I with it, and as if we ought to be grateful to each other and so shake hands to say farewell. And already the new waits at the door along with my faith . . . that this new thing will be the right thing, the last right thing."[6]

We must understand that the virtue of this cure lies in the fact that every time we adopt a new habit, we believe it's the right one and that it will last forever, that we have found a way to overcome boredom and hyperactivity alike, with the sense of relief of the man who has finally returned home and can set down his bags. Enduring habits thicken the atmosphere and shrink our space for movement, whereas brief habits enlarge it, furnish it, and embellish it. "To me the most intolerable, the truly terrible, would of course be a life entirely without habits, a life that continually demanded improvisation—that would be my exile and my Siberia."[7]

AKRASIA, OR THE COUNTERFEIT DISEASE

ACTION IS THOUGHT of as something spontaneous; of irrepressible forward momentum; a kind of gust of wind; of elementary propulsion; a motor that, like all motors, benefits from carrying out only two simple functions: start and stop. The blueprint for action is the same obeyed by all engines of locomotion: begin, execute, end. It is a blueprint that implies that to want is to do; to wish is to be able.

But ask anyone who wants to stop snacking or go to bed earlier and is unable to do so to come forward and testify as to the visceral dysfunction of willpower, whereby the will is dissociated from the ability and breaks the circuit of action. Not being able to do what one wants, finding that one's willpower lacks will, is a form of illness. This pathology has been cataloged since antiquity under the name "akrasia"—the modern version being known more commonly as procrastination.

A Cry for Help

Today's the day I get it done. . . . Well, all right, tomorrow then. In a matter of seconds, the will has yielded, abdicated, quit. Unable either to begin or to finish, we stall, delay, convinced that there will always be another time when we will have the strength to act. The akratic patient lives in the there-and-then, a vague and distant destination that never seems to arrive. His present is never-ending and diluted; it flows on unhindered by date or deadline, forever putting off the moment of action. There are joyful akratics and tormented akratics. One may never get down to work, convinced of her ability to bring it all together at the last moment; the other may be burdened by the guilt of always deferring to another day and by the painful awareness of all that needs to be done and never is. The former risks suffering an acute attack of exhaustion, since last-ditch efforts are never good for the cardiovascular system; the latter is chronically fatigued, using all her energy to obsess over all she has failed to accomplish, her mind weighed down by the magnitude of her ever-growing to-do list. The former teeters on the edge of the abyss—time to turn it in, pay it, answer in two hours—whereas the latter lives in a perpetual state of grinding subjugation to her *needs*—I need to change the lightbulb, I need to fill out the job application, I need to buy my plane tickets, I need to lose five pounds. . . . Both are perpetually stressed; according to the experts, the stress is not the result of not knowing what to do but of knowing exactly what to do but not doing it.

That is akrasia: a weed that never stops spreading, that invades our life and muddles its contents, like continuous feedback in our sound system, a kind of grueling stasis. I am not the person I should be because I do not do what I should be doing. Procrastination is not so much a dysfunction of the will, incapable of accomplishing what it has set out to accomplish, as a diminishing of the self, an inability to be oneself, trapped in an existence that is neither dead nor alive. Saint Augustine provides the best diagnosis of the disease: "I all but enacted it: I all but did it, and did it not: yet sunk not back to my former state, but kept my stand hard by, and took breath. And I essayed again, and wanted somewhat less of it, and somewhat less, and all but touched, and laid hold of it; and yet came not at it, nor touched nor laid hold of it; hesitating to die to death and to live to life."[1] A conflict is playing out between my resolve and my actions, a crack in my soul that makes my life a kind of semi-existence, making me a stranger to myself and shaping self-knowledge into self-hatred.

Diagnosis

The conclusion that Saint Augustine draws is that our liberty is a "counterfeit liberty," capable of desiring but incapable of willing that which it desires.[2] The solution must therefore come from elsewhere, from an exterior source of assistance, since it would be ridiculous and futile to turn to the will to overcome . . . a lack of willpower. This external, supplementary will is what Christian theology calls grace. The question of whether the human will remains free when it can act only by virtue of divine grace is one that engaged the greatest minds and unleashed the fiercest cultural battles of the seventeenth century, from Pascal through Fénelon to Racine. The challenge is not purely theological; it is to determine whether humankind is free or if "will" is just a word, referring to no reality, if we are moved to act solely by our pursuit of pleasure.

And yet we still have the option of heroism, of the person who knows herself to be counterfeit but also knows that this infirmity does not prevent her from battling. From that perspective, life is seen as a war against oneself, from which the critical motivation is to emerge the victor. As Plato frames it, "the first and best of victories, the lowest and worst of defeats—which each man gains or sustains at the hands, not of another, but of himself; this shows that there is a war against ourselves going on within every one of us."[3] It takes the kind of heroism imagined by Corneille to go to war against yourself and, like the Cid, to coin a principle for action that is the exact opposite of akrasia: "I did what I must: I do what I must do."[4] It takes the heroism of Medea, which is in itself the sweetest of her victories:

NÉRINE

Your country hates you, your husband is faithless—
When all is lost, what is left to you?

MÉDÉE

Me, I say.
Myself, and that's enough.

Nérine

What! You alone, madame?

MÉDÉE

Yes, in me alone you see fire and flame,
And the earth, and the sea, and hell and heaven,
And the scepter of kings, and the thunderbolt of the gods.[5]

But you might also opt for the Ulysses method, which consists of winning . . . by refusing to fight. Armed with a feeble will, we are indeed certain to lose. Like Ulysses, then, it might be better to lash yourself to the mast so as not to succumb to the song of the sirens.[6] It is wise not to count on willpower to defeat the will; it is more effective to withdraw from the realm of voluntary action, which most certainly will prove to be of little help, and to resort to a mechanism or prosthesis, such as bindings and a mast.

The more brutal and uncompromising the method, the more effective it will be. Force yourself, handcuff yourself, prevent yourself, muzzle yourself—anything you can do to substitute for a will that has no willpower. Rather than choose to eat only three pastries don't eat any at all, be sure to pay your bills, go on the installment plan. . . .

Pascal's Automatic Method

Akrasia is linked to the powerful hold that the present moment has on our will, which is always stronger than any future benefit. Sure, smoking kills . . . but not right away. Right now, I want a cigarette. If we rely exclusively on our willpower, it will always be defeated by instant gratification. It is therefore advisable to substitute the automatic for the voluntary—to behave the way we dive, allowing no time for reflection or hesitation by imped-ing or short-circuiting any freedom of movement, which for the akratic person always ends up being an excuse for delay. One may also ask one's friends to play the role of whip-cracker, like Charles de Gaulle, who informed his chief of staff about his de-sire to quit smoking so that he could play the enforcer. The solu-tion cannot come from within; you can't fight a lack of willpower with your will.

Victory is far more assured by recourse to automated solu-tions that brook no delay or excuse. "For we must not misunder-stand ourselves; we are as much automatic as intellectual," Pascal reminds us. As a result, actions undertaken reflexively succeed "without violence, without art, without argument" where an effort of the will would have been in vain. The will "acts slowly, with so many examinations, and on so many principles . . . that at every hour it falls asleep, or wanders." On the other hand, automatism, the self-imposed reflex gesture, acts "in a moment, and is always ready to act."[7] Paying bills, making calls, filling out forms, making reservations, replenishing stocks, all the things we never get around to starting—you have to do them without thinking, immediately, the way a machine would do it. *Done. Next.*

BURNOUT

WHOEVER HAS NOT two-thirds of his day for himself is a slave, be he otherwise whatever he likes, statesman, merchant, official, or scholar."[1] Thus wrote Nietzsche. It's not your job that matters but how much time you have to yourself. We are buying time for ourselves when we work, but the problem is that work takes up all our time. That's the tragedy of the proletariat. The absurdity of Sisyphus's situation, doomed to roll his boulder to the top of the hill, only to see it roll back down every time, is the absurdity of the salaried condition in which you have to work to live and, for the very same reason, you spend your life working. There is a kind of mundane and silent despair in having to "earn your bread," to spend your life (or at least your week) waiting to live. It's the Friday night syndrome, when we finally feel as if we're alive.

Work makes you stupid because it inherently prescribes a compulsory dose of repetition and treading water. Competence is very often nothing but the fruit of these accumulated repetitive gestures. All work is equally servile, requiring our submission to deadlines, a boss, relationships, results. Some will object that they love their work, but that is not enough to suppress its elements of constraint and subservience; it's only that, in this particular case, pleasure has the upper hand, or the job is on easy street.

Hospitalization

"Have a great weekend!" The expression rings out like a freedom cry, a flip of the bird to the enemy, but it also carries a burden of anxiety, because we will have to live an entire lifetime in the coming forty-eight hours, rebuild from the ruins of our alienated office existence a life that is at long last free. Squeeze all that we are, everything we love and desire into the cramped and paltry space of those two days. And if we feel obliged to spend the few hours we have to ourselves on distractions and partying, isn't that the same servitude we find at work? "What are you doing this weekend?" I claim my right to do nothing at all, to be unproductive, inept, good for nothing. A nobody. A zero. No investment, no goal achieved, no supply, no demand. No bookkeeping; life in the red. Defying the logic of the to-do list, letting time flow by without measure or fraction, without beginning or end. Without a schedule.

Yet some people claim to "actualize" or even to "outdo" themselves in work, to demonstrate "competence" and "expertise," asking in return only that their efforts be "recognized." But what is it they want to be recognized? Themselves? Their status? Their results? Others say that the struggle for recognition is a way of humanizing work, of curbing its tendency to depersonalize and distance the salaryman from the decision-making process and the creative aspect that may come with exercising a profession. That it's a way of co-opting the right to be oneself during the workday. While this may be commendable in principle, it has also given rise to an orgy of performance assessments and infantilization. Moreover, in the struggle for recognition we may overlook the need to resolve real problems: equal pay for men and women, improved information sharing, the validation of merit over seniority, better-organized meetings, and so on.

Treatment

Work is alienation. In an early work, Marx uses this concept to define the laborer's condition. Work is always external to us, imposed, even if we are able to decide how to perform it and even if we know how to do so. In that sense, all work is forced labor. It is alienation, too, because it does not satisfy a need but is the means to satisfy needs external to itself (travel, clothing, vacations, etc.). The alien character of work "emerges clearly in the fact that as soon as no physical or other compulsion exists, labor is shunned like the plague. External labor, labor in which man alienates himself, is a labor of self-sacrifice, of mortification. . . . As a result, therefore, man (the worker) only feels himself freely active in his animal functions—eating, drinking, procreating. . . . What is animal becomes human and what is human becomes animal."[2] The most "creative" part of ourselves expresses itself not in work but in consumption, in which we get our vengeance and, we believe, are able to be ourselves, choose, decide, distinguish ourselves.

Work is the rule of necessity, the animal and primitive compulsion to survive and to secure the means of subsistence. Civilized man certainly no longer spends his days in search of his daily bread, but he does spend the greater part of his time working to meet his needs. The only liberation possible will come not only from "shorter working periods,"[3] but also from, still according to Marx, the abolition of the division of labor and the assignment of each individual to a unique occupation. "[I]n communist society . . . nobody has one exclusive sphere of activity." You can be a plumber one day, and a professor of philosophy the next, "hunt in the morning, fish in the afternoon, rear cattle in the evening, criticize after dinner. . . ."[4] But we then run up against the paradox that work is both that which alienates us and that which defines us. How many encounters and conversations begin with the question of what we do in life, what profession we practice? How, then, can we ever hope to be able to abolish work itself?[5]

The remaining solution is not a collective but an individual one and, according to Nietzsche this time, consists of fighting, for the sake of our health and our moral equilibrium, everything within us that makes us a good worker: punctuality, zeal (or competence), obedience (availability), and effectiveness (expertise). It is only at that price that we have any chance of protecting what we are from the contamination of the salaried life.

Nietzschean Reeducation

Anyone who works is his own hangman. In this realm, we always do too much, that is to say, more than what we are remunerated to do. Every salaried person is in a certain way selfless, and therefore exploited. Whatever work you do, work is inherently distinct from what you are; it is a discipline flaunted as a virtue that breaks down and alters our individuality. Thus, the qualities it demands of us, such as diligence and obedience, are in reality hardships that we inflict on ourselves.

Every worker ends up being the victim of his work. Every job is not a vocation but a sacrifice in which we lose ourselves by honoring that which is demanded of us: "One praises the diligent even if he should harm his vision or the originality and freshness of his spirit; one honors and feels sorry for the youth who has 'worked himself to death.' . . . Too bad that the sacrifice is necessary! It would surely be much worse though if the individual . . .

had considered his own preservation and development more important than his work in the service of society!'"[6]

We are always overgenerous in giving of ourselves to the work we do. In this field, we must learn to be a bad employee and to fight against all manifestations of zeal, which is the engine of alienation.

"Man Is Wolf to Man"

THE THING THAT defines love and friendship is the special miracle of the encounter. It establishes a before and an after; it somehow calls into existence, simultaneously, the self and the other. It makes us feel that before we met Paul, Vincent, Clarisse, or Marie, we were forlorn, a little lost, a little hesitant, whereas now we know just where we are. We are rediscovered.

In the social world, contrarily, we do not encounter the other because it is everywhere, physically or symbolically, embedded in the law, regulations, prohibitions and obligations, contracts and conventions. The other does not does not come to meet us; it was there before us, it is right in front of us. We make way for it: "After you, I insist." That is the modality of the social "encounter."

Clinical Profile

Imagine what our lives would be like without the rules of the road: a free-for-all, sexist and violent, dangerous and primitive, where all speech is insult, every street is a corridor of death, and every stranger in his turbocharged sports car is an enemy who takes no prisoners. Without traffic lights, stop signs, and rights of way, our streets and roads would be battlefields. A war of each against all.

Without shared, coercive rules, competition among vehicles and for destinations would lead to bloodshed. Why should I yield to anyone else? Nothing's forcing me to, nothing about him calls for or deserves my consideration. After all, we're all equal, every driver is just as worthy as the next. There's nothing to suggest I need to curb my desire to move along, to arrive, to drive. Life without rules of the road is precisely what Thomas Hobbes describes as the state of nature—the state we would be in if we didn't live in society, that is, in an organized system of rules and interdictions.

Diagnosis

Man is not naturally cruel, but he seeks naturally to satisfy his desires, and that forward momentum leads him to view others as obstacles and even rivals. While man may be an "arrant Wolfe"[1] to man, it's not out of some congenital barbarity but because he's tormented by the need to attain his ends. Why would anyone obstruct that natural freedom, which amounts to the right to get whatever I desire? It's my right. The problem is that my neighbor claims the same right for herself. How then can we arrange things so that right does not lead to war, desire is not lethal, and the freedom of one person does not threaten that of others? The solution is the stop sign. In other words, the law.

Without established laws, there is nothing to stop me from going all out to get whatever I want, from exercising my due right. This is a democracy, after all. But it takes the compulsion of law to ensure that my right is neither threatened nor threatening. The law is thus the opposite of the right—of the right I claim to do as I please. That is actually the genuine meaning of democracy or republic. Life in a society requires me to waive my unlimited right over everything and all things, so long as everyone else does the same. This amounts to a transfer of power, because that right becomes vested in the state, a representative, a monarch, a president. That is how we agree to do away with personal dictatorships and tyrants, and that we ensure security for all.

The difficulty then lies in preserving individual liberty within a society. Do we need a police officer on every corner or civic education? Do we need a strong executive power or participatory democracy? Is it better to be free or to be safe? It is when we're behind the wheel that we are best able to understand the great questions of political philosophy.

Leviathan

It is not the wolf that man has feared since time immemorial; it's man himself. And it's to guard against the danger that he poses to himself in his own eyes that he turns to power, the main function of which is protection: "[T]he essence of the state . . . is mankind's fear of itself,"[2] writes Friedrich Engels. Society nullifies relationships based on power and fear, transforming the other from an enemy into a neighbor. In order to overcome the evils attendant on keeping company with our peers, we need to establish an absolute power. Whether that sovereign power belongs to an individual or an assembly makes no difference; what matters is that it usurps all other powers unto itself, and in particular the right claimed by individuals to do whatever they want: "[D]uring the time men live without a common Power to keep them all in awe, they are in that condition which is called Warre; and such a warre, as is of every man, against every man. For WARRE, consisteth not in Battell onely, or the act of fighting; but in . . . the Will to contend by Battell."[3]

That was Hobbes's solution in the seventeenth century, and today we are still able to discern its founding principles in our own rules of the road. If we did not assign to a sovereign power, established over the individual citizen, our presumed right to do whatever it takes to obtain whatever we want, we would live in a state of insecurity and permanent belligerence. The Leviathan, both a political beast and a social machine with a monopoly on sovereign power, thus serves to preserve us from that tyranny that we would instinctively exercise over one another, and allows us to sleep in peace.

FEAR AND TREMBLING

WHAT ARE WE afraid of? The list is a long one, from great terrors to little frights, from the fear of others to the fear of death, not forgetting the anxiety of failure. Fear seems to imply the idea of punishment and guilt, as if we had done something wrong and would have to pay the price. To a certain extent, all fear is the fear of retribution. It must therefore imply a belief, howsoever vague or even unspoken, in a hidden providence presiding over our destiny, handing out gold stars or demerits.

Ultimately, then, all fear is somehow fear of the gods, whether they take the form of a superior force deciding our fate or of human beings to whom we ascribe superhuman powers—as we might to a boss, a spouse, or a philosophy professor. . . .

Symptoms

Stress is everywhere. It is no longer a disease; it's a way of life. Everybody is stressed and everything is stressful. The full spectrum of our emotions comes together under the term; feeling anything at all is a kind of stress. Falling somewhere between excitation and apprehension, stress defines anything that disturbs or flusters us. Should I see John? Stress—whether John is my lover, my dog's vet, my impresario, or my union rep. Should I go to Belgium? Stress—whether it's for a business trip, a holiday, or language study. "Stress" is a generic term to designate any activity, to describe any feeling. Fear has given way to stress; it has somehow been diluted, applicable to everything and nothing, to the benign as to the critical. It has also become more clinical, medicalized, and medicated; associated exclusively with neurobiology and stripped of its existential dimension. From the brain to the stomach and back, stress no longer has that quasi-religious resonance that used to be associated with fear. It is no longer either dread or paralysis; it is merely dysfunction.

But any remedy we might consider for stress would have no effect on fear, which cannot be reduced to the reaction of our neurocerebral system to an external danger. Fear is not stress, and no effort to calm the one will succeed in soothing the other. Indeed, fear comes down to something more basic—to the fact that we are visible, exposed, naked to the world and in a life over which we have very little mastery. Fear is linked to the fact of being seen.

It is fear of the gods, who are the embodiment of our acute awareness of being seen, and thus of being seen in a bad light. Ever since the first Homo sapiens had the idea of standing up, we have lived in fear, which is expressed in timidity, anxiety about the future, or the dread of being abandoned.

Remedy

Fear—the direct result of being "exposed," visible, and helpless—always contains a dimension of paranoia and superstition. Paranoids and the superstitious alike are dominated by fear, leading them to overinterpret everything, imagining omens and threats in the most trivial of events and attributing meaning to the most anodyne gestures. They are constantly watchful because they are constantly being watched. The superstitious man is not afraid of others but of some larger other, of ill-defined identity, that observes him and presides over his fate. From religion, all that he has retained is the fear and trembling, projecting his internal anxieties onto the external world. His fear is most closely linked to the concept of the unconscious championed by Freud: "What he considers hidden corresponds to the unconscious with me, and the compulsion not to let chance pass as chance, but to explain it as common to both of us."[1]

Unlike the psychoanalyst, however, the superstitious man has no understanding of unconscious motives; he displaces them into the outer world, ascribing to chance or bad luck that which, in actuality, is the exclusive product of the psyche. We can decode not only fears but also mythology and beliefs, by identifying their psychological causes: "[A] large portion of the mythological conception of the world which reaches far into the most modern religions is nothing but psychology projected into the outer world. . . . We venture to explain in this way the myths of paradise and the fall of man, of God, of good and evil, of immortality, and the like."[2] Our fears encompass the archaic, superstitious, and paranoid concept of a world where nothing is fortuitous or accidental, but where everything is managed by gods or invisible forces.

In many respects, Freud is a philosopher of the seventeenth century. In his analysis of superstition and paranoia, which we believe to be the two modalities of fear, he recapitulates the theses formulated by Spinoza, for whom the primary task of philosophy was to free us from superstition. What we attribute to fate, the gods, or hoodoo, and which fuels our fear—both of punishment and of being in the wrong—is dependent on rational causes that can be identified and defined. There is no other reality than the link between cause and effect that governs all things—humankind, the world, history, and our individual existence—and does so with the impersonality and systematicity of the laws of mathematics. We are not watched but determined. The only god is that of causality.

The Spinoza Method

We are afraid because nothing in life seems to be certain: "[L]ike waves of the sea driven by contrary winds we toss to and fro unwitting of the issue and of our fate."[3] Fearing shipwreck, we ceaselessly vacillate between hope and anxiety, apprehension and confidence. In this continuous uncertainty, we nurture all sorts of fears and grasp at the most insignificant "sign": If men "could govern all their circumstances by set rules, or if they were always favored by fortune" they would never be ruled by superstition."[4] The Spinoza method is a radical one. It demands that we understand things by their causes and not by our fears, that we substitute knowledge for superstition, to replace the anguish of uncertainty with the joy of knowing.

"It is the principle on which politics is founded, since nothing influences the people more strongly than superstition."[5] Because fear is despair and hope is fearful, men "flail around, now hoping for better things and then fearing worse ones, without having any real reasons."[6] The fearful man is always alone in that he has no inner resources; rejects reason; and gives in to anger, hatred, and depression.

All people, and not only the religious and the credulous, are vulnerable to superstition. It is the principle on which politics is founded, since "nothing influences the people more strongly than superstition." It is what leads them to to worship their "kings as gods."[7] A free person, who seeks always to identify causes and not to ward off bad luck, is focused on what must be done and not on what must be feared. Her "wisdom is a meditation of life"[8] and not of fear.

We must therefore strive to subject our fears to purely rational treatment that ascribes causes to them that are not necessarily reassuring—finding reassurance in an uncertain world is all but impossible—but manageable. If a tile falls on a passerby in the presence of a black cat, the first thing to do is call a roofer.

LOVE

LOVE IS A passion of the body and of the soul. It's a combination of blood, nerves, and performance. Intellectual and sensual, when it causes pain it's both physical and mental. According to Julien Hayneufve, a seventeenth-century French Jesuit writer, it is "the queen of passions"[1] to which all the others are subordinate, and on which they feed and depend. What is avarice if not love of money? Ambition, if not love of power? Joy, if not love of life? All our passions are aspects of love (or hatred). But just as these passions become hallmarks of individuality, determining particular traits and defects (calculation, arrogance, irascibility, altruism, meanness), so the passion of love seems to apply to all people without distinction. Everyone has been in love and suffered for it at one time or another. Everyone has experienced in more or less the same way the feeling of possessiveness that defines passionate love. Love has, at one time or another, enflamed and enslaved us all.

How do our emotions come to be so corrupted? Inherently benevolent, attentive, and generous, how does love turn possessive, melancholic, and alienating?

For if love is a disease of the soul, that is because it is a disease of freedom, the experience of possession and dispossession of the self—in the words of Immanuel Kant—"an enchantment . . . that refuses to be corrected"[2] or healed. We never feel more alive than when we are in love, but at the same time we no longer belong to ourselves. That is the intoxication brought on by the poison of passion.

Symptoms

In all passions we find some aspect of the thrill of the game: a self-contained universe, reduced to almost nothing—a roulette wheel, odds, evens, woman, man. The intensity of the bond reduces the world to a binary pulsation: presence, absence, being with John, being without John. I think, I speak, I want, I don't want—I do all these things just as I did before, like the able-bodied person I once was, but now they all have but one object and objective: John. The intensity creates its own one-dimensional universe; romantic passion is a strong emotion but, for the same reason, it strips the real from its own reality, turning everything that is unconnected to passion into a ghost. Loving is a kind of mania. The impassioned person is a monomaniac. Passion is both a mental construct—"I think only of her"—and a verbal one—"This is what she said to me, this is what I'll say to her"—from which life has somehow withdrawn. Monolithic and immense, it depopulates and polarizes. Her, me. The world, its movement, the animation of life, its unanticipated dangers and nuances all cease to exist. Love stories are as monotonous as plot points: he told me, I saw him, she answered . . . and yet, this emotional clockwork appears to be fully alive, significant, irreplaceable, desirable, beloved, and loving.

Black-and-white yet delighting in trivial details, fixated on the grandiose yet tilting toward sentimentality, the romantic passion makes us ill not only at its climax but throughout the course of its infection, through the insatiability and restlessness to which it condemns us. It's not only that we can never get enough when we are in love, it's also that we literally want to devour the other. And those who have best expressed that truth are not the novelists but the philosophers.

Parallel Medicine: The Kantian Remedy

Kant does not hesitate to compare romantic passion to cannibalism: "[W]e never find that a human being can be the object of another's enjoyment, save through the sexual impulse."[3] To love is to wish to "ingest" the other; sex is a "crime of the body."[4] Love is by its very nature cannibalistic, and sexuality merely manifests that truth about passion. It is not only sex without love that can be compared to appetite, it's all romantic feeling. In *Phaedrus*, Plato first alerted us to such anthropophagy, in which the wolf loves the lamb just as the lover adores his beloved, and desires with all the fondness of a beast of prey.

The solution offered by Kant to save oneself from such ingestion is marriage. While it may not stop romantic cannibalism, it does legalize it by replacing predation with a relationship framed by the provisions of the law. Marriage is an exercise in domestication, which civilizes the savagery of passion. It ushers us into a realm that is regulated and tempered by the law, where each spouse is contractually authorized to use the other sexually on the condition that both acknowledge the fact that the other is a person with her or his own wishes and feelings. In that sense, every marriage is a marriage of reason, in which the law limits and rationalizes desire and its voracity. Outside of marriage, we are nothing but a slab of meat when we are beloved.

But modern times have seen the rise of the love marriage,

which effectively imports emotional cannibalism into the pacified precincts of marriage. It's the wolf in the sheepfold, the predator in bridegroom's clothing. It introduces the problems of fidelity and the persistence of desire. We should be able to love the way pigeons love one another, serving as each other's entire world, here and everywhere, forever and now, creating through love a universe as vast as the real one, rivaling it in all its exoticism and seasons, as envisioned by the French poet Jean de la Fontaine:

> There were two pigeons on a tree,
> Who loved each other tenderly.
> One, in his folly, tired of home,
> Resolved in distant lands to roam.
>
> . . .
>
> Let happy Lovers wander if they will,
> But only to the neighbour hill:
> Let one be to the other's thought
> A world of beauty, never twice the same,
> Each all in all to each, the rest as naught.[5]

Philosophical Remedy

Since love is vulnerable to infection and toxins, most often through the agency of jealousy, betrayal, dependence, and the extinction of its own flame, we must find the means to survive it. If we do not care to subscribe to the marriage solution, we still have the wandering Venus therapy prescribed by the Epicurean poet Lucretius. Compared to the sections of *De rerum natura* devoted to love and its ravages, everything else seems a little staid. His recommendation is a radical one: we must flee romantic passion, which renders us fatally stupid and unhappy. Stupid, because love is blind, or rather it exults in its own flaws.[6] Being in love is like worshipping at an altar, ascribing superhuman qualities and a supernatural or divine nature to the person in question.

To love is like taking vows; we love because we long for the ideal and we need to believe in the existence of gods and goddesses. Romantic love makes us unhappy because it wants the impossible—it wants both to ingest the beloved and to lose itself in him. But not even the craziest or most symbiotic devotion can ever make one plus one equal one. We remain irremediably two, distinct from each other, which in and of itself gives weight to the danger that we will one day be separated.

Wandering Venus Therapy

To cure ourselves of love, we must . . . fall in love. We must love another, maybe even the first guy to come along, so as to free ourselves of the illusion of exclusivity that fuels passion—John, the one and only, the unique. We must stop telling ourselves "Because it was he, because it was I" and start telling ourselves "There are other fish in the sea, I got along just fine before this." Even the most powerful love is merely the outcome of a happy coincidence; there were others before, there will be others to come. "It behooves . . . to vent the sperm, / Within thee gathered, into sundry bodies, / Nor, with thy thoughts still busied with one love, / Keep it for one delight, and so store up / Care for thyself and pain inevitable."[7]

In addition to the mirage of exclusivity that leads you to believe that in losing a beloved you will lose the ability to love, the romantic passion, as we have seen, tends toward cannibalism. With their lips and their teeth, lovers seek to devour one another, to literally incorporate that which they desire. "For they hope / that by the very body whence they caught / the heat so love their flames can be put out. / But nature protests 'tis all quite otherwise."[8] This is indeed a unique instance where need is not fulfilled but strengthened by its satisfaction—we can neither possess the other nor completely lose ourselves in her. As a result, the more we love, the less we are sated. "Greedily their frames lock, / And mingle the slaver of their mouths, and breathe / Into each other, pressing teeth on mouths—/ Yet to no purpose, since they're powerless / To rub off aught, or penetrate and pass / With body entire into body." Their embrace carries a whiff of vengeance against the other, who attracts while resisting: "For, lo, the ulcer just by nourishing / Grows to more life by deep inveteracy, / And day by day the fury swells aflame." The lovers thus "waste away / With unseen wound."[9]

There's no significant difference between happy loves and unhappy passions, sexual desires and feelings—all of them are debasing, all of them make us ill. "And the woe waxes heavier day by day—/ Unless thou dost destroy even by new blows / The former wounds of love, and curest them / While yet they're fresh, by wandering freely round / After the freely-wandering Venus, or / Canst lead elsewhere the tumults of thy mind."[10]

Lucretius's epicurean cure is not about being tirelessly libidinous—he is not recommending such an epileptic Venus—but about learning not to pin on love the illusion of having found the one and only, the unique, or to believe that we can only love but once.

LOVE AT FIRST SIGHT

I SAW HIM, he saw me, I fell in love with him instantly, fiercely, for no reason, without a single word being exchanged. How can we explain love at first sight? This inflaming of desire with no apparent cause? What is the mystery of an attraction that makes you feel as if you know everything about a person in a second, as if in fact you have always known and awaited him? Descartes was the great scholar of love at first sight and explained how it functions. Contrary to the enduring philosophical legend, this phenomenon is proof of the close link between body and soul that Descartes consistently championed, his *cogito* being not pure mind but mind capable of falling in love at a glance. In *Passions of the Soul*, he recounts how, as a child, he loved a young girl with a slight squint. This love made such an impression on him that forever after he felt a special affection for any one with a similar countenance.

We are attracted to a certain kind of man or woman because we have already been so in the past, going all the way back to childhood, without having preserved a conscious memory of it. The connection that was established at that time between the feeling of love and such and such a physical quality—or even defect, such as the strabismus described by Descartes—at a later time ensures that the mere sight of the same characteristic will irresistibly unleash desire, like a Pavlovian reflex. Love at first sight is thus not a meeting but a reunion. I saw him and fell in love because I have always loved him. Love at first sight is a muscle memory transferred to the soul.

Prescription: A Cool Head

The remedy for love at first sight and boiling passion is to keep a cool head. Since we are susceptible to being attracted to defects, we must remain vigilant and subject the object of our passion to a detached, dispassionate assessment. To that end, we need to allow time for the fever to subside and for the emotions that have heated our blood to abate. And above all, we need to remember that passion exaggerates, that, as Descartes explains, it leads our souls astray, strengthening our reasons for pursuing the object of our passion and weakening our reasons for avoiding it. The only solution, therefore, is to wait for it to pass, since all passions by definition pass, after which a more reliable assessment of the object of our desire can be made.

You do not confront a passion head-on, you do not reason with an attraction. You must only be patient and allow the psychophysical combustion to fall to a normal temperature. For life is possible only in a temperate zone, to which our episodes of emotional superheating always return.

If Charles Swann had only followed Descartes's advice, he would not have squandered the best years of his life in loving a woman who, despite not even being his type, drove him mad with love the first time he met her: "To think I've wasted years of my life, that I wanted to die, that I felt my deepest love, for a woman who didn't really appeal to me, who wasn't my type!"[1] Confirmation of Descartes's superiority over Proust.

OPIUM SMOKERS

KARL MARX ASSERTED that religion is the "opium of the people,"[1] a system of beliefs with the power to ease suffering and deaden consciousness. All belief is an escape from reality, an aspiration to artificial, and hence illusory, paradises. For to believe is to nurture illusion—illusion about the reality of your own situation and what you can reasonably hope for. Belief is a pathology of hope that leads you to wish simultaneously for too much and for too little: too much, when it denies reality; and too little, when it is unable to effect change.

Our opium dens are not designed to promote action. They respond to a unique need—the need to be consoled. Reality is what it is—the unvarnished truth—but beliefs, utopias, myths, and ideologies are all ways we have found to console ourselves over it.

Addictology

There is no Santa Claus. Our emergence into adulthood is built on the ruins of that archetypal belief, but as adults we tend to replace it with others, be they formulated by a political party, a social circle, a school of thought, or a supermarket. The death of Santa Claus is caused by a lethal nosedive into the real, prosaic, and disenchanted world. Presents do not come from a workshop in Lapland but are purchased in the store down the street. Exiled to reality without compensation or reparations, we never fully recover. But in the beliefs of our maturity we will continue to seek that primordial consolation, now forever beyond our reach.

This need for consolation is complemented by the urge to be like everyone else—and make no mistake, even eccentrics and minorities conform to norms. Everybody belongs to a group, whose patterns of behavior, speech, eating, and thinking we adopt more or less consciously. Middle-class Catholics, millennial hipsters, intellectuals, or outcasts, we all lay claim to being both universal and different. We telegraph our differences—white, black, woman, man, and so on—through the "values" we embrace, which we expect to be acknowledged by all and sundry. These values, which we wear to identify ourselves and stake our claims to ownership, whitewash reality and seek to pass off social and cultural constructs as normality. "A man has more practical sense than a woman." "Women are gentle and intuitive." "It must be true since I heard it on the radio." As Marx puts it, "men have constantly made up for themselves false conceptions about themselves, about what they are and what they ought to be. They have arranged their relationships according to their ideas of God, of normal man, etc. The phantoms of their brains have got out of their hands. . . . Let us liberate them from the chimeras, the ideas, dogmas, imaginary beings under the yoke of which they are pining away. Let us revolt against the rule of thoughts."[2]

Our social affiliations require us to behave like everyone else, or rather like those in our own group. They ensure that individuals "find their conditions of existence predestined, and hence have their position in life and their personal development assigned to them by their class, become subsumed under it."[3] What we take for reality is merely the product of our (social) outlook on the world. Ideology speaks before us and for us; all we do is echo. We are the derivative product, the parrots of prefabricated opinions. Ideology is thus a psychosomatic illness whereby our values induce behaviors, tastes, and language and determine the way we see ourselves. We somatize these social codes, more often than not subconsciously, and it is precisely when we believe that we are thinking for ourselves that we are channeling those with whom we identify—the femme fatale, the captain of industry, the perfect mother, or the woke activist.

Diagnosis

Nevertheless, we require make-believe in order to live and act. We need the support of myths and symbols to confront reality, to make the world less unsettling, more familiar. But such make-believe can ossify into ideology, where it's no longer about the great questions—questions about creation, death, and fate—but about having an answer for everything. Ideology doesn't think; it asserts through ready-made slogans and formulas. Yet, at the root of this perversion of the imagination, we still find a belief in paradises, lost or to come: nature, the Golden Age, El Dorado. . . .

We know very well that perfection is impossible to achieve, that it is extraordinarily difficult to be the best, and that all action entails disappointment of some sort; but we need to believe that we will be offered consolation, that the bad guys will be punished and the good guys rewarded. We could not endure reality without such utopias. We must therefore encourage escapism, restore the power of myth and the life force of fantasy.

The Blumenberg Diagnosis

Our relationship with reality is never direct, serene, or temperate. We are only able to face it by prevaricating. As the twentieth-century German philosopher and intellectual historian Hans Blumenberg put it: "The human relation to reality is indirect, circumstantial, delayed, selective, and above all 'metaphorical.'"[4] We encounter the world through stories and myths. Turning the world into metaphor strips it of its indifference and makes it more acceptable, livable, and intelligible. "All trust in the world begins with names, in connection with which stories can be told."[5] We need to tell ourselves stories in order to allay our fear, the primordial dread of being thrown into a world without certainties or safe havens: "Stories are told in order to 'kill' [*vertreiben*] something. In the most harmless, but not least important case: to kill time. In another and more serious case: to kill fear."[6]

Religion, philosophy, culture in general constitute a kind of self-help program designed to overcome our fear of reality by populating it with myths and stories: "It cannot be taken for granted that man is able to exist. . . . I see no other scientific course . . . except . . . to destroy what is supposedly 'natural' and convict it of its 'artificiality' in . . . the elementary human accomplishment called 'life.'"[7] We need the assistance of every artificial paradise and every imaginary construct just to survive.

Nowadays, tourism undoubtedly trumps culture in playing this function of escapism and consolation. In traveling the world, we stave off the fear it elicits. We are at home everywhere and reality is neither harsh nor absurd but exotic and welcoming. There is still the risk, however, of contracting the chronic tourist's disease of infecting the unknown with the known.

REGRETS AND REMORSE

THE SUFFERING BORN of regret is barely endurable. It creates a distance between you and life that nothing can ever bridge, because what is done is done and what is left undone must forever remain so. Life does not allow do-overs or catch-ups; it barely gives us enough time to think. Everything we do is both unconditional and definitive—a kind of improvisational dance with destiny.

Whether we regret something we have not done or have remorse for something we have done, in either case the mind comes up against the irreversibility of time, which makes all action irreparable and gives it a kind of eternal dimension—now and forever, the harm has been done and cannot be undone.

We may look for excuses, but nothing will erase the words that went unspoken or those that ought to have remained unsaid. Nothing, except forgiveness, which alone has the power to put an end to regret. But are we able to forgive ourselves? How do we absolve ourselves of our own misdeeds? Better yet, how do we avoid making them, how do we avoid having to rue who we are and what we have done?

Consultation

I should have taken that job two years ago, I shouldn't have said that yesterday, I ought to have accepted, I should have refused . . . All those yeses and noes we were unable to say, all those "if onlys" that torment and fill us with guilt—they all carry a burden of bitterness and sorrow. To regret is to deviate from the route of one's own life, to languish in its byways, to loiter in its dead ends and uncharted territories. This accumulation of nothingness, faults, and errors induces a kind of paralysis; it benumbs and petrifies us. We have lost ourselves and our loss can never be recouped. Regret is an acute form of unhappiness because it forces us to acknowledge the irrevocable and the irreparable—the accident that changed everything and can never be reversed.

We have lost our innocence, that carefree certainty that we are doing the right thing, that we own our lives and are masters of our behavior. Exiled from our own lives, we endure our unremitting frustration without ever being able, as the French poet Charles Baudelaire put it, to "kill the long, the old Remorse / That lives, writhes, twists itself / And mines us as the worm devours the dead."[1] More often than not, we choose to take it out not on ourselves but on others—life, society, the world at large, and John in particular. We blame them for not having given us our due. That is how remorse turns into resentment and envy.

Remedy

The world of regret (that which will not happen) and the world of remorse (that which ought not to have happened) are worlds without hope. Fate rules over all our actions there; they are destined, absolute, and irrevocable. They straitjacket our existence as in a narrow corridor without doors or windows, with no options other than the things we have done or failed to do. We are chained to a present moment that unfolds ineluctably from the mistake that has been made or the opportunity that has been squandered. We hope for nothing—neither for a second chance nor for anything new to come along. The sorrow of despair is the most painful of all; it holds our future hostage, exiles us from the present, and fossilizes our past.

We must find a way to reintroduce the principle of hopefulness into such frozen lives. Not by nurturing dreams and nostalgia but by acting. Hope is action. It is not wishful thinking or a vague desire. To act, even in the humblest of fashions, is always to hope—that is, to fight back against the irrevocable, to defy the irreversible. It is to create something new, to open a fork in the road. It is the only way to avoid being mummified by irreversibility, sadness for what will never return, or the pain of what should not have been done.

The Montaigne Remedy

"When I dance, I dance; when I sleep, I sleep. . . . There is good husbandry in enjoying it: I enjoy it double to what others do; for the measure of its fruition depends upon our more or less application to it."[2] Montaigne does not encourage us to abandon ourselves to the present moment, to totally immerse ourselves, and relish it blissfully. Quite the contrary; he urges us to remain vigilant and to intensify our experience by being mindful of it: "I ponder with myself of content; I do not skim over, but sound it."[3] By this method, the mere fact of being alive becomes a form of action. Indeed, even in sleep we should be able to stay active, aware of our selves and of our feelings.

The brief and irreversible span of our lives is thereby profoundly transformed. Action—that is, the fact of complementing our lived experience by the will to live it to the full—imbues the ephemeral with an intensity that it would not otherwise possess: "I will stop the promptitude of [time's] flight by the promptitude of my grasp; and by the vigor of using it compensate the speed of its running away."[4]

It boils down to living your life the way you practice your profession: with diligence and expertise. This is in no way related to carpe diem–style nonchalance; it is a discipline, almost a kind of labor. Not an art but a craft, the modest ability to compose with the means at hand, without attitude or stage direction. Ordinary life thus assumes the allure of a glorious masterpiece. In that context, the act of sleeping is no more inconsequential than dancing—everything is me when I engage and apply myself to it. The only real obstacles to this appropriation of time are fatigue and illness.

To free ourselves of regret and remorse, we must therefore live deliberately, with intelligence and, to some extent, with effort. The secret of a deliberate life is to always remain as close to yourself as possible, master of your experience, and not passively submit to external events. We must act to avoid regret and submission. Not to do whatever we will but to will whatever we do. Only then will we find that "There is nothing so fine and legitimate as well and duly to play the man . . . and naturally to know how to live this life."[5]

THE WORRIES OF
EVERYDAY LIFE

TRAGEDY OR COMEDY, good luck or bad, everything is a matter of rhythm. A life reduced to a few moments retold at rapid-fire tempo—I was walking, there was a car . . . I met him at the book club, he loved me, he cheated on me, I cried—borders on farce. The same misadventures related in detail and at a measured pace become solemn and dramatic.

But the tempo of life is rarely that of a great symphony, all tremolos and rubato; rather, it is made up of the trills and quavers of our everyday worries, that endless buzzing of ordinary concerns, like flies that pester us on even the most lovely summer days. They won't kill us, but they leave us feeling constantly irritable and hassled as we go about our business.

Not so much catastrophes as problems—money, the neighbors, the office—these thousand little indignities, breakdowns, and annoyances form the droning baseline of our days. They take possession of our mind, weigh on our stomachs, and limit our movements. They are the polluted air that we often breathe, eroding and hobbling our freedom.

MONEY

THE LOGIC OF money is brutally binary—you have it or you don't. There's no place here for the nuances of free interpretation; either you have one hundred dollars or you do not. To be sure, the amount in question means different things depending on whether you're rich or poor, but it's still what it is: one hundred, two zeros after a one. It has the unwavering solidity of dogma; like it or not, that's the way it is, and it's the same for everyone—one hundred dollars is one hundred dollars. More stubborn than a fact and less open to interpretation than a value, money has the immovable and compact nature of an object: a stone is a stone, a fifty dollar bill is a fifty dollar bill.

But unlike a stone, money can buy everything and anything. Of all objects, it is the only one that makes every transformation possible, while remaining exactly what it is. One hundred dollars can transform itself into perfume, plane tickets, taxes, gasoline, jars, and jam, and can even bring in more dollars. Money is the only object able to appropriate other objects, not by creating them, as a tool would, but by making them appear as if by magic.

It's that special magic that turns our needs into products. When you have it, it becomes the intermediary between desire and reality. *I want, I buy, I own.* Better yet, it is the sleight of hand that turns anything you want into a reality. *I dream of Corsica, I have a plane ticket for Rome*. Through the omnipotence of money, my yen for Corsica is no longer an unfulfilled desire but an awaiting reality. Endowed with the spectacular power to fill a void, its ability to contribute greatly to our happiness is easy to understand. There are few things that will not evolve from a state of representation into one of reality through its agency, and happiness itself is among those abstract notions that money can make real. "For me," Karl Marx tells us, money is "the *other* person,"[1] because it mediates almost all my relations with the world and other people. As a result, without money, we have neither a place in the world nor any kin; we are stateless and asocial.

It is a reality within reality, in that it does not depend on our opinion (again, one hundred dollars is one hundred dollars, no matter what you think about them), and yet it's also the entry fee that gives us access (without it, nothing or almost nothing exists for us; even our feelings need money to exist, display themselves, and endure). From an economic-political angle, we can say that money, when it comes in the form of a salary—that is, work performed in return for sustenance—is a modern form of servitude. Upon consideration, it is an unsustainable paradox that the very means we need to survive must be paid for at the cost of our own existence.

Against all odds, it is the practice of metaphysics that best illustrates the omnipotence of money. And it's in the highly technical and abstract context of proofs of God's existence that the dollar, or its equivalent, enters the realm of philosophy. In his *Critique of Pure Reason*, Kant turns to money to highlight the insurmountable difference between idea and reality. The classic proof of God's existence, as developed by Descartes, rests on the idea of God. The idea of a perfect, infinite, and all-powerful being necessarily implies that she exists, because how could a being be perfect if she were not endowed with the primary perfection of existing? The very definition of God thus supposes her existence.

For Kant, however, we can't gloss over the idea of existence so blithely; God doesn't exist simply because we have an idea about God. Real existence is something more than any mere idea we might have about it. It cannot be proven on the basis of a simple definition. Thinking about one hundred dollars—is not at all the same thing has having one hundred dollars. Anyone, even the most mathematically illiterate among us, would have to agree with Kant on that. It is when they are in your pocket, not in your mind, that one hundred dollars become real. "But in reckoning my wealth there may be said to be more in a hundred real dollars than in a hundred possible dollars— that is, in the mere conception of them. For the real object—the dollars—is not analytically contained in my conception, but forms a synthetical addition to my conception."[2]

Existence comes into play only in the course of concrete experience (that in which I touch or see my hundred dollars): "[W]e may as well hope to increase our stock of knowledge by the aid of mere ideas, as the merchant to augment his wealth by the addition of noughts to his cash account."[3] We can no more conclude from the idea of God that she exists than we can increase our real wealth by jotting down a series of zeros on a piece of paper. A thing can be said to exist only if I have experienced it. And that is how money brings the magnificent edifice of metaphysics crashing down. Nothing can resist the reality of money because nothing can be deduced from it—not even God. It should be noted that Kant displays a dismissive consistency in always linking religion to money, since he also affirms that misers are usually bigots.

Prescription

It may be objected that Kant's example is poorly chosen and that, as a result, his reasoning doesn't hold up. In effect, the empirical, concrete existence of one hundred dollars can hardly be compared to the existence of God. They are not of the same nature. At the heart of the proof, the existence of God is not an empirical but a theological necessity. If God is indeed God, she can exist, and not merely in thought, only in the minds of those who are capable of formulating a logical proof. What kind of God would she be if the certainty of her existence was accessible only to metaphysicians? She would be merely a God of philosophers, a paper divinity. The reality of God's existence is more real than that of money. That is what such proofs seek to demonstrate in showing that this existence is not a mere belief or representation but an absolute fact as tangible, and perhaps even more so, than the dollars in my pocket.[4]

So there is in fact one area in which money does not work its magic—that is, the area of metaphysics, and in particular the proofs of the existence of God. For in this particular case, real existence arises directly from the idea one entertains of it: to think of God is to think that she exists. It is in God's nature that she must exist, without which she would not be God but simply a person whose existence is contingent (I might not have existed, just as my parents might not have existed, and so on). Strictly speaking, metaphysics could be justified in stating simply that God is God, and therefore she exists.

More than disinterest and selflessness, which consist of withdrawing from the world and waiving its laws, in particular those of buying and selling, metaphysics has the power to subvert mercantile logic by turning a simple representation (God) into the equivalent of reality (her necessary existence). Metaphysics is a world turned upside down, in which reality resides more in ideas than in facts, where that which is most evident is to be found less in what can be seen than in what can be thought.

In this realm, the binary logic of money (either I have it or I don't) does not hold sway. If time is money, in metaphysics time is abstracted from the rule of money. Nothing is more anticapitalist than spending ten minutes practicing metaphysics.

NEIGHBORHOOD PROBLEMS

WE DO NOT live alone, which is both our good luck and our tragedy. This time, Kant is right: man is a sociopath whom we have forced to socialize. All societies are founded on "the unsocial sociability of men, i.e., their propensity to enter into society, bound together with a mutual opposition which constantly threatens to break up the society."[1] It takes very little for our social veneer to be disturbed by our innate revulsion of our neighbor. The other is truly other, he who is unlike me, who impedes my freedom of movement and disturbs my leisure. He coerces me and opposes me.

But it is this opposition "which awakens all his powers, brings him to conquer his inclination to laziness and, propelled by vainglory, lust for power, and avarice, to achieve a rank among his fellows whom he cannot tolerate but from whom he cannot withdraw."[2] If hell is other people, it is also the arena of culture; it is indeed through contact with our fellow man, for whom we have so little fellow feeling and whom we cannot bear yet cannot do without, that we develop our talents, our tastes, our moral compass, and even our character.

The Porcupine Syndrome

Social life, then, is bought at an extortionate price, built on a foundation of unsociability and mutual disgust. This ensures that any relationship, even the happiest, contains a seed of animosity that we repress or conceal out of politeness, as manifested by the quarrels that break out among associates, the resentment of a subordinate for his superior, the irritations aroused by our partners or by a child in her parents. Our relationships flow less from an inherent inclination to sociability than from an inability to endure solitude.

We seek out the company of others for the same reason we travel or we drink: to beat back the exhaustion of being ourselves. As Schopenhauer puts it, "people band together to offer [boredom] a common resistance."[3] We need to be mindful of this bargain we make when we agree to live in society. We swap our personal emptiness and lack of inner resources for both the aggravations and the fleeting gratifications and diversions delivered by other people— our friends, loved ones, children, and colleagues.

We are all victims of the porcupine syndrome, against which the sole remedy is to learn how to keep our distance. "On a cold winter's day a community of porcupines huddled very close together to protect themselves from freezing through their mutual warmth. However, they soon felt one another's quills, which then forced them apart. Now when the need for warmth brought them closer together again, that second drawback repeated itself so that they were tossed back and forth between both kinds of suffering until they discovered a moderate distance from one another, at which they could best endure the situation—This is how the need for society, arising from the emptiness and monotony of our own inner selves, drives people together; but their numerous repulsive qualities and unbearable flaws push them apart once again."[4]

The correct distance that makes social life tiring yet bearable is that which is established and ensured by courtesy. "Keep your distance" is the guiding principle of a sociability that causes us no pain and by which we cause no pain to others.

THE BORE, THE PYGMALION,
AND THE SOLILOQUIST

HERE ARE THE three greatest social pests: the bore, who drowns us in trivia, be it about his grandchildren, the state of his intestines, or his latest vacation; the Pygmalion, who dispenses—preferably to the benefit of women, whose education, as everyone knows, always needs refreshing—lessons about things and about life, with that confidence of imbeciles, who can be recognized, as asserted by Thomas Aquinas, by the fact that nothing intimidates them ("*Omnes stulti* [. . .] *omnia tentant*"[1]); and lastly, the soliloquist—generally a woman, her male equivalent being the bore—whose only mode of conversation is the monologue. All three suffer from intellectual pathologies as well as a social defect—they all lack the capacity to arouse interest in their listeners.

Knowing how to interest someone is knowing how to persuade them, as opposed to contradicting and quibbling, which many take as a sign of intelligence. Persuading is very simply having something to say—something that acts as a key to unlocking new perspectives, new angles that allow us to see things differently. It is nothing less than the equivalent, in everyday conversation, of Kant's synthetic a priori judgment: an unexpected connection arising neither from a contradiction of what has just been said nor from haggling over the fine points, but is an unprecedented affirmation that no one had thought of and that causes all listeners to say "Of course!" Something that originates in both surprise and logic, that convinces and entertains. Nothing grandiloquent—a modest yet subtle argument. Whoever lacks this talent can only be a bore.

It would be a mistake to underestimate the contagious nature of conversation. As Montaigne frames it: "It is impossible to overstate how much [our mind] loses and deteriorates by the continuous commerce and contact we have with mean and ailing ones."[2] We have to acknowledge that the only thing that interests us is ourselves, and that, other than ourselves, we only have one or two topics of conversation that are worth our while. We are like an instrument that produces only one or two sounds. We need to extend ourselves in order to supplement this monotony; we need other people to create the illusion that ours is a rich and fascinating personality. Which is what makes us both so boring and so sociable.

The Penalization of Boredom

"We die in proportion to the words which we fling around us,"[3] the Romanian philosopher E. M. Cioran explains. We wear ourselves down with chitchat, we kill ourselves with all our empty and repeated words. We believe that we're engaged in an "exchange of ideas" when in fact we are merely trading in insignificance. "And if we meet others, it is to degrade ourselves together in a race to the void, whether in the exchange of ideas, schemes, or confessions."[4] We don't know how to deal with silence or with solitude. "Life is only that impatience to . . . prostitute the soul's virginal solitudes by dialogue."[5] We bloat ourselves with information and words. But nothing can mask the fact that we are insolvent, that, as Schopenhauer puts it, we have nothing "which can compensate either for [the] boredom, annoyance and disagreeableness"[6] we experience in company and in conversation.

The solution in this case is not therapeutic but penal—we must punish the tedious. That is the radical method championed by Montaigne—we must either flee the bores or sanction them. "Your ignorance and obstinacy cost you last year, at several times, a hundred crowns."[7] If we are unable to steer clear of them, we must tax those who pontificate, soliloquize, and fatigue us. And we, too, must pay some sort of stupidity tax for the monologues and flaccid disquisitions we inflict on others.

We must either outlaw or punish conversations that lead nowhere, that are built on systematic contradiction, that drone on about trivial inanities: our kid's measles, parking problems, the advantages of such and such a package deal, the impropriety of such and such a practice, and so on. According to Montaigne, these are true "verbal crimes," to which we might add the tendency to traffic in muddled ideas, ready-made phrases, pedantry, and vanity. Some minds are like tree stumps, from which "there is nothing to be had or to be expected."[8]

But yet again, it is our own selves that we must put most severely to the smell test. "Had we a good nose, our own ordure would stink worse to us, forasmuch as it is our own."[9] For every criticism aimed at others we must aim another at ourselves, and ask whether we are not guilty of the defect we deplore in them. In our conversations, we must demonstrate backbone, not obstinacy. Get in your digs, but do it in a spirit of playfulness, not of superiority. You can also fall back on silence, which has the advantage of making you look smart: "To how many foolish fellows of my time has a sullen and silent mien procured the credit of prudence and capacity!"[10]

(OTHER PEOPLE'S) CHILDREN,
FRIENDS, AND FAMILY

WHY DO PARENTS feel obliged to talk so loudly, to practically shout at their children in public places (the bus, the movie theater, the restaurant, the train) as if inviting the whole world to profit from the life lessons they claim to be giving? These parents are convinced that everything they tell their children deserves to be heard, that it's their civic duty to broadcast their schooling to the public. They feel imbued with an importance that the others, the childless, do not enjoy; they have a civilizational mission that cannot be fulfilled in whispers. Apparently, education is improved by being shared with bystanders.

It's not only parents and their children who are capable of disturbing our tranquility; sometimes it's the entire family. Descartes had such a phobia of his family's attentions that he often stashed a packed bag in a hidden place in preparation for a quick getaway: "The great many friends and relatives whom I was compelled to see stole all the time and leisure I devote to the studies that give me such pleasure."[1] Even our friends can enfeeble our intellects.

In response, Montaigne tells us, we must cultivate "a friendship that pleases itself in the sharpness and vigour of its communication, like love in biting and scratching."[2] If it is to be interesting, friendship, like love, must draw blood. Sentimentalism sedates and kills. It's healthy to reject consensus and to welcome conflict. We spend time with our friends not because we enjoy agreeing with them but for the singular pleasure of arguing with them.

The Platonic School

It is a popular notion that children should be the very picture of innocence. But there is a germ of cruelty in children that no amount of socially acceptable language and proprieties can fully domesticate, something that resembles a beast of prey, that slumbers within us and that we are unable to subdue. It is that primordial predatory nature that we see in children and that parents cannot muzzle.

The Platonic solution may well seem extreme to some, in that it recommends entrusting the education of children to the community: "[T]he wives of our guardians are to be common, and their children are to be common, and no parent is to know his own child, nor any child his parent."[3] Children will belong to no one, or rather, their education will be a matter of state.

It is, indeed, a thing too important to entrust to parents alone: "You know also that the beginning is the most important part of any work, especially in the case of a young and tender thing."[4] In this Platonic scheme, mothers, who are able to procreate from the ages of twenty to forty (up to fifty-five in the case of fathers), will be tasked with nursing, which "shall not be protracted too long,"[5] without attempting to determine whether the child at their breast is their own. They will not be in charge of caring for their own children, who shall be assigned to child-care professionals to attend to their needs.

Social cohesion depends on the suppression of the family, for nothing entails more discord and antagonism, and undermines the state, than educations based on differing principles.

BOSSES AND COLLEAGUES

WE SPEND OUR days navigating between deference, flattery, and subservience. The world of work, despite being regulated by laws and policed by supposedly civilized behavior, remains a world of voluntary servitude. We agree to bend to rules whose justification is not readily apparent. The basis of wage labor is a service contract whereby the servant rents his ability to work to a master. His freedom is preserved, however, because the contract is based on his consent to work and the contingent nature of the commitment. But how, in such circumstances, is the individual worker not reduced to an object, a good that can be bought or rented? While a services and facilities agreement, as it is known, prohibits forced labor, it nevertheless does not prevent a certain kind of voluntary slavery. We cannot help but recognize that business retains an element of this original serfdom—we rent ourselves for a salary. And in renting our skills, our time, and our knowledge, we consent to sacrifice a part of ourselves, of our individuality, for insertion into the hierarchy and the smooth functioning of the whole.

Every salaried person has a little court jester in her, a little chief who is subservient to power yet yearning to share in it. For power is not organized in a binary connection between dominant and dominated; it is available to everyone, with each of us hoping to grab it and exercise it. As the sixteenth-century French philosopher

Étienne de La Boétie demonstrates in his 1576 *Discourse on Voluntary Servitude*, we are all "supporters of despotism."[1] It is never a single individual tyrannizing all the others; it's an entire system of "petty chiefs," the lieutenants, accomplices, and courtesans of the despot, who "gather round him and support him to have a share in the booty."[2] It is the aspirations of the little tyrants that ensure the durability of even the least legitimate or most incompetent power. All of us, petty chiefs that we are, are "always on the watch, ears open,"[3] greedy for our share of power. If we submit ourselves voluntarily, it is because we hope in turn one day to compel submission.

Radical Solution and Intermediate Solution

One radical solution for eradicating the regime of voluntary servitude within the world of work is that proposed by Marx. It consists of the suppression of salaried work, a source of alienation and division. Some people maintain that Soviet communism was but one stage toward the establishment of such a classless society without wage labor. It is hard to see, through all the coercion and privation, what happiness the full establishment of communism might have hoped to offer. According to Paul Lafargue, Marx's son-in-law, who believed that "all [the proletariat's] individual and social woes are born of its passion for work,"[4] the solution is to create a society of idleness, leisure, and restricted working schedules of five to six hours a day. The proletariat must "return to its natural instincts, it must proclaim the Rights of Laziness, a thousand times more noble and more sacred than the anaemic Rights of Man. . . . It must accustom itself to working but three hours a day, reserving the rest of the day and night for leisure and feasting."[5]

But we see the secondary effects of this solution every day in the fact that leisure itself ends up being experienced as work, as if we were incapable of doing anything at all in a lighthearted way, as if we were compelled to inject everything we do with the spirit of earnestness that we bring to the business world. Everything—travel, museums, entertainment—is work to be checked off.

One apparently less radical solution is that of escape, elaborated by the twentieth-century French surgeon, neurobiologist, writer, and philosopher Henri Laborit in *Éloge de la fuite* (*In Praise of Escape*). Power, he tells us, is bad for the health. "Escape is the only course that allows us to remain normal with respect to ourselves, so long as the majority of men who consider themselves to be normal strive in vain to become so by seeking to assert their dominance, be it individual, group, class, national, international, and so on." In effect, neuronal medicine demonstrates that "the activation of the pituitary gland and the adrenal cortex, which if maintained results in the visceral pathology of so-called psychosomatic diseases, is a phenomenon linked to those who are dominated, those who seek without success to establish their dominance, or those who are dominant but whose dominance is challenged and seek to maintain it." Such behavior, related to the seizing or exercise of power, is strictly speaking abnormal, for there is nothing normal about suffering from "stomach ulcers, sexual impotence, arterial hypertension, or the kind of depression-related syndromes that are so common these days." Stable and unchallenged dominance being so rare, if we wish to remain normal and healthy—that is, not to suffer from the pathology of submission or from that of domination—our only choice is to "escape as far as possible from hierarchical competitions."[6]

Centuries before the advent of the neurosciences, Pascal also advocated escape as a social strategy that he called keeping "our thought secret."[7] This form of inner resistance consists of respecting the hierarchy while giving it little or no thought. If you wish to maintain your freedom in the kingdom of deference, you must learn to bend only the knee and not the spirit. We attribute to those who dominate us talents they do not possess, transforming them into stars or idols. This practice has even penetrated politics, turning the servants of the State into *personalities*. We must not scorn men of power but respect without admiring them; we must obey in appearance while never kowtowing intellectually.

When engaged in the pursuit of power, it's a good idea to hold on to a "secret thought" that forbids you from ascribing any kind of real superiority to your hierarchical "superiors" or even to yourself. Such secret thoughts represent the best defense against any inability to see the big picture and any blind and automatic attraction to the external symbols of power. "To the greatness of [social] institution we owe the respect of institution, that is, certain external ceremonies . . . but which do not make us conceive any real quality in those whom we honor after this manner. It is necessary to speak to kings on the bended knee. . . . It is a folly and baseness of spirit to refuse to them these duties."[8] Yet it's an error of a different order to admire those who have reached the pinnacle, and have done so more through entitlement than talent. For we must always remember that "We do not choose as captain of a ship the passenger who is of the best family."[9]

GETTING WET AT THE POOL, AND OTHER THINGS YOU CAN'T CHANGE

OUR RELATIONSHIP TO the everyday, and perhaps to life in general, is more often than not conducted at the level of complaint. Our most consistent gripes concern the things we can't change: our noisy neighbors, Monday mornings, working for a living, watching our children grow older and our parents age, the squandered opportunity that will never return. It all comes down to complaining about getting wet when you go to the pool. As the Greek Stoic philosopher Epictetus teaches: "When you are going about any action, remind yourself what nature the action is. If you are going to bathe, picture to yourself the things which usually happen in the bath: some people splash the water, some push, some use abusive language, and others steal."[1] It's exhausting and futile to get upset over what cannot be otherwise and to wish that things were other than they are. Telling yourself "that's how it is" will always be a winning strategy. It's therefore better to know what to expect and to accept it than to seek vainly to alter the course of events.

And since, in a certain way, every desire is a desire for the impossible, the will to modify what cannot be modified, it is critical to learn to desire only that which can be obtained. Anything beyond that must be held to be without interest: "But, for the present, totally suppress desire: for, if you desire any of the things which are not in your own control, you must necessarily be disappointed."[2]

The *Sustine et Abstine* (Endure and Abstain) Treatment

Even when we are happy, we can't help wishing for another reality, two or three little things more, one or two little details less. But for the sake of our peace of mind, we must learn to accept whatever life offers us: "Remember that you must behave in life as at a dinner party. Is anything brought around to you? Put out your hand and take your share with moderation. Does it pass by you? Don't stop it. Is it not yet come? Don't stretch your desire towards it, but wait till it reaches you. Do this with regard to children, to a wife, to public posts, to riches, and you will eventually be a worthy partner of the feasts of the gods."[3] That is the lesson proposed by the great Stoic master Epictetus: learn to want what you can have.

We are neither puppets nor gods, but just because we don't determine the rules of the game doesn't mean we can't play well. What we are able to obtain is neither good nor bad; very simply, it doesn't concern us in any way. We must learn to count it as nothing—as neither interesting nor desirable. What happens to us will happen to us whether we like it or not. We must therefore hope for whatever happens to us and want whatever we hope for not to happen.

> We are not the authors of our lives but merely actors within them: "Remember that you are an actor in a drama, of such a kind as the author pleases to make it. If short, of a short one; if long, of a long one. If it is his pleasure you should act a poor

man, a cripple, a governor, or a private person, see that you act it naturally."[4] All we can do is to rise to the role we must play: "For this is your business, to act well the character assigned you; to choose it is another's."[5]

But if all we want is what is possible, can we even call that desire? Isn't there, contrarily, a kind of anxiety and hopefulness in desire that make us perpetually dissatisfied with what is and always seeking what is not?

AFFLICTIONS OF THE MIND, TEMPORARY AND CHRONIC

CONTRARY TO WHAT is often imagined, the Stoic sages and their Epicurean cousins are not carefree nightingales focused on singing of the beauty of the present moment. Horace, the Epicurean poet who coined the famous adage *Carpe diem*, also speaks of the "dark worries" that grip humankind, and the Stoic Seneca does not conceal the "disgust with life and the world" that often seizes him.

There are indeed moments when we feel lost, when the world feels like an alien place, and when the life we are leading feels like that of an exile. The evidence of our everyday existence—me, here, now—is shattered and everything appears absurd and baseless. Things speak to us in a language we don't understand. We become prey to depression, also known as melancholy, taedium vitae, or acedia.

We are also vulnerable to sudden infatuations, jealousy, and envy that obsess and inflame us in a kind of foretaste of the hell that may one day await us.

DEPRESSION, MELANCHOLY, TAEDIUM VITAE, OR ACEDIA

IN APPEARANCE, NOTHING has changed—you still feel like yourself, you have two arms, two legs, the same lower-back pain, the same voice, and the same memories. But the truth is, nothing is the same; everything you are—past, present, and future—feels like a series of empty rooms that have just been vacated in preparation for a move. And there you are, surrounded by cardboard boxes, not knowing whether to stay or leave. It's not your zest for life that has disappeared—doesn't that vanish every Monday morning and even several times a day? It's your attention to detail, the little nothings that make up your day, a mix of habits, pleasures, tastes, and perceptions: a very hot cup of tea with a wisp of milk; the neighbor upstairs, watching the nightly news at full blast; Paris when the air is almost fresh and pure in the morning; the evening that lies ahead; and sometimes the bright moon hovering in the kitchen window. . . . It's your day-to-day life that disappears with depression.

You find yourself face-to-face with life, plain and simple, with what it means to live and to exist. Face-to-face with the task of being—a concept that has fascinated philosophers for so long. But this state of being no longer has any description or occupation, no preferences or focus; you just *are*, in a way that is almost abstract.

Before you lies an existence without defining qualities, a present without momentum or end. Depression is an illness of the present: it stretches out unbroken, uniform, and final, like the stillest of lakes. This sadness of being is a state not of paucity but of overabundance; you have too much of everything—time, the present moment, your surroundings, your very life—but nothing gels, nothing abides. It's all there, flat and slack, without rhythm or history.

That is the definition of depression, according to Seneca, who, like the other Stoics, considered it to be one of the most violent of the passions, "that tossing to and fro of a mind which can nowhere find rest."[1] It is an absence not so much of energy but of curiosity; nothing attracts the attention, nothing beckons, our existence has been bled dry of all detail. In Baudelaire's reckoning, "no days so lame as all the days I know / while, crushed by years of ever-falling snow, / boredom, dull fruitage of my apathy, / waxes as vast as immortality"[2] You are alone, frozen while others are in motion, "lost in a misty desert," "forgot by all today,"[3] without a home or a season, condemned to a present as broad and blank as eternity, as if it will never come to an end.

The Monk's Remedy

Acedia was wreaking havoc in the monasteries. The term was a neologism coined by the hermit Evagrius Ponticus in the fourth century to designate a disorder characterized by aimlessness and frustration, the ancestor of depression, also known as the noonday demon because it tended to attack the monks at that time of day when time seemed to stretch out to infinity, when nothing seemed capable of disturbing its slow, relentless course. No landscape is lovely under the midday sun, which allows neither shadow nor relief. Equal parts torpor and anguish, according to Evagrius the demon of acedia is "the most burdensome of all the demons. It besets the monk at about the fourth hour (10 am) of the morning, encircling his soul until about the eighth hour (2 pm). . . . Then it makes the monk . . . look round in all directions in case any of the brethren is there. Then it makes him hate the place and his way of life and his manual work. It makes him think that there is no charity left among the brethren; no one is going to come and visit him."[4]

For another fourth-century monk, Saint Nilus, this melancholy provokes both "a feeling of privation and a driving hunger."[5] You want something anxiously and impatiently, but you don't know what it is. You are burdened by your thoughts, but they never lead to action or to clearly formed ideas. You mark time.

You might opt for the drastic remedy identified by Saint Rudolf, which consisted of suspending himself by the arms with ropes attached to the ceiling, while reciting psalms, in order to ward off torpor—which corresponds to Evagrius's highly recommended technique of *antirrhetikos* ("talking back"), which overcomes the vacuum of boredom by filling it with speech and words (from the Bible, in this case). Evagrius advises readers never to trust in the judgments and ideas that come to mind at such moments, and Ignatius Loyola likewise recommends making no sudden changes at times of desolation, but to abide firmly and consistently by prior decisions. The best thing is to do precisely the opposite of whatever your apathy tells you to do.

The best remedy, however, remains manual labor. In the fourteenth century, a practical guide for monks, the *Fasciculus Morum*, contrasted acedia to the "holy work" of laboring, sowing, reaping, making beer, cooking food, cutting and sewing clothing, building houses.

Manual labor is essential, because all other tasks fray the nerves and leave the mind to its own devices, with no specific object on which to focus its attention. Manual labor has the advantage of having a beginning and an end, which helps to dissipate the emptiness of boredom and the apathy of idleness. *Doing* distracts temporarily from *being* at precisely that moment when simply being is difficult and feels dull and pointless. Concentrating on something external to yourself marks off a breathing space where you can anchor yourself and try to master the depressive nausea that makes life seem both too long and too empty.

ENVY, JEALOUSY, AND SCHADENFREUDE

THE GRASS IS always greener somewhere else, just because it happens to be anywhere else. It starts in high school, maybe even earlier, when a classmate has curly hair while yours is straight, the trendiest schoolbag when yours is a supermarket knockoff. Later, the same girl will go on to wear high fashion and marry the handsomest boy in class. Later still you'll find her at the office, on vacation, slender as a rail in her bikini on the beach at Le Touquet, at banquets and teas, with her precocious children and husband better looking than ever. Envy is based on an apparent violation of the principle of equality—you see a peer leading a life that you believe should rightfully be yours but is pointedly not. Why her and not me? Don't I have as much right to it as she does? This de facto inequality against the backdrop of equal rights is felt as an injustice; you envy the other because you feel aggrieved.

Jealousy, on the other hand, is a disorder not of equality but of exclusivity. You want to be the be-all and end-all of the other; his past, present, and future; his world, his life. Which implies that nothing he has belongs to him—not his desires, his gaze, his relationships. Everything he experiences fuels jealousy because it is something he is keeping to himself. You are jealous of his friend, his joys, his thoughts, his dreams, his entire being.

Wicked joy, or schadenfreude, is not jealousy but the unhealthy pleasure you derive from the misfortunes that strike those you envy. It is a kind of malevolent admiration, a reverse sympathy whereby you commiserate over the pain of others so as to better enjoy it. It's the sacrilegious resolve to see the idol destroyed and the gods brought low.

Freud's Sublimation Cure

The solution proposed by Freud to loosen the grip of envy is based either on "suppression" or on "sublimation," and in both cases through a process of censorship. What we call our conscience is really nothing more than suppression, an attempt to prevent our impulses and unconscious representations from manifesting themselves. The ego is a suppressed entity, endlessly blocking the way of our emotional triggers and our psychic makeup. It is a superficial being, submerged, the only presentable and decent part of who we are: "[M]en are not gentle creatures who want to be loved, and who at the most can defend themselves if they are attacked; they are, on the contrary, creatures among whose instinctual endowments is to be reckoned a powerful share of aggressiveness. As a result, their neighbor is for them not only a potential helper or sexual object, but also someone who tempts them to satisfy their aggressiveness on him, to exploit his capacity for work without compensation, to use him sexually without his consent, to cause him pain, to torture and to kill him. *Homo homini lupus* ['Man is a wolf to man']."[1]

It is our destructive impulses—*eros*, the sexual impulse, and *thanatos*, the aggressive impulse—that life in society and the civilizing process as a whole require us to sacrifice, or rather to retool, convert, and sublimate into more altruistic, more "refined" relationships. Life in society is nothing more than an exercise in inhibiting our constitutive aggressiveness. Our "nature" is worked over and re-built in order to make us capable of enduring other people. Envy or schadenfreude are thereby domesticated, although they continue to pose a constant threat to our relations with others. Rather than allow our destructive desires to express themselves, we invest their energy in less antisocial, more peaceful activities, such as writing a book of philosophy, joining a book club, hiking in the mountains. . . .

And even so, what we take for liberation is just another way of mastering our impulses. The twentieth-century German sociologist Norbert Elias, cites the evolution of bathing manners as an example of this. "Only in a society in which a high degree of restraint is taken for granted, and in which women are, like men, absolutely sure that each individual is curbed by self-control and a strict code of etiquette, can bathing and sporting customs have this relative degree of freedom develop. It is a relaxation which remains within the framework of a particular 'civilized' standard of behavior."[2]

The evidence for the malign joy of schadenfreude lies in the fact that every pleasure carries within it a seed of ferocity and primitive aggression. Joy is not a pure emotion; it can be experienced in response to someone else's failures, in the wicked enjoyment we derive from watching and wallowing in them.

The emotional universe is not one of peace and love; its skies are darkened by disturbing clouds and its atmosphere is suffused with the reeking miasmas of resentment and jealousy.

LIFE'S LITTLE
ACCIDENTS

LIKE IN ALL good Westerns, what gives our lives their moments of greatest dramatic tension is the confrontation between good and evil, moments of intense suspense when we must choose between acting wisely and acting wickedly, between being the good, the bad, or the thuggish.

Whatever the origin of values may be, whether there is such a thing as absolute good or merely mutable, relative social conventions, the instant when we need to decide how we will act is critical. To tell the truth or to lie? To return the fifty-dollar bill that has just fallen from the pocket of its rightful owner, or to discreetly palm it? To defend a colleague who has been unjustly mistreated or to keep silent? We are the theater of bitter confrontation between that which suits us and that which commands the respect of others. And our conscience finds itself more often than not to be a guilty one.

MISTAKES, SINS, AND A GUILTY CONSCIENCE

WE ARE THE battlefields of silent wars in which two armies clash but usually end up declaring inglorious cease-fires. Our inner life seems to continuously ring with the clamor of these clashes between good and poor behavior. The refrains are always the same: "Must I?," "Can I?," "What should I do?" We tend to believe that the conscience can never be anything but clear or guilty, and that morality is imposed on us like a promise that we are bound to keep, leaving us torn between disgrace and courage, shame and integrity. There is a kind of pact between humankind and the law that requires individuals to take a stand on moral issues. While this awareness does not make angels of us, it can nevertheless be the basis of a guilty conscience and fuel our sense of failure, of not having behaved as the goodness within us dictates. Morality prescribes above all that we keep our promise to be the vehicle through which goodness enters the world.

Moral behavior establishes a new timeline, creates a break in the ordinary course of self-interest and egotism. At the very moment when it is undertaken and as long as it persists, it effectuates a kind of salvation—the world has been saved from what it might have been without the possibility of goodness. Doing good constrains and obligates us, weighs upon us and chastens us, but it also reveals what we are capable of. Moral duty tends in an upward direction and confers a power that we did not know we possessed. A clear conscience is not the halo of the righteous but the satisfaction of having acted beyond self-interest. It may also be the product of fear of punishment, for morality also acts like a kind of internal judge. As Kant would have it, "Every human being has a conscience and finds himself observed, threatened, and, in general, kept in awe (respect coupled with fear) by an internal judge; and this authority watching over the law in him is not something that he himself (voluntarily) *makes*, but something incorporated in his being."[1]

One might certainly challenge Kant's assertion by noting that the essence of morality, the definition of what is good and what is evil, is determined by cultural and social factors. The fact remains that the critical moment when we are called on to act morally is a face-to-face confrontation with ourselves, a hand-to-hand duel between the self and the conscience, which "follows him like his shadow when he plans to escape. He can indeed stun himself or put himself to sleep by pleasures and distractions, but he cannot help coming to himself or waking up from time to time; and when he does, he hears at once its fearful voice. He can at most, in extreme depravity, bring himself to *heed* it no longer, but he still cannot help *hearing* it."[2]

Anything we do while turning our back on what we would selfishly prefer to do is both an imposition and an act of celebration. There is a kind of moral narcissism in this tribute that virtue pays to itself. I can look at myself in the mirror, and do so with the joy that goes with a clear conscience. There is a moral theater, a stage that we take when we act morally, imagining ourselves under the gaze of our conscience, in the mirror (or the camera) of our soul. That's why Socrates is right to say that it is better to suffer wrong than to do wrong, because it is better to be at odds with the entire world than with oneself.[3]

The problem is that we come to terms with our conscience too easily: "I didn't understand . . . Yes, but . . . You should have said something . . ." We make excuses and procrastinate ("Next time . . . When I can . . .") to keep guilt at arm's length and delay fulfilling our promises. This phenomenon, which psychologists call "cognitive dissonance," consists of finding good reasons for bad behavior ("I'm honest but . . ." "It's not my thing, but . . ."). In this way, we attach greater weight to our own welfare than to that of others, and to the welfare of our loved ones than to that of our neighbors or strangers, and we favor instant gratification over delayed. We tailor the moral world to our own figure, rejecting any constraint or sacrifice that good behavior might entail. Partisans of the path of least moral resistance, we cultivate the art of lying to ourselves.

In this scenario, people are malicious not by design but only out of moral laziness, thanks to the petty accommodations we make with our conscience. To behave badly is to act as if we were invisible to others and to ourselves, as if no one were able to see our behavior, and hence to judge it. The wicked person acts out, on her own behalf, the myth described by Plato, according to which the shepherd Gyges came into possession of a magic ring. As soon as he realized that the ring allowed him to be invisible, "he contrived to be chosen one of the messengers who were sent to the court; whereas soon as he arrived he seduced the queen, and with her help conspired against the king and slew him, and took the kingdom."[4] The wicked man does not have a guilty conscience. Making himself invisible, he behaves as if his actions will not be judged harshly either by others or by himself. The feeling of omnipotence that this arouses in him is easy to understand.

The Categorical Imperative Treatment

Omnipotence will not be swayed by our cognitive dissonances—all those yes-buts and the exceptions we allow to the moral standard—unless we raise the bar by imposing ethical requirements that are stricter than the "normal" in order to compensate for our tendency to justify ourselves. If we wish to be a little bit moral, we have to be mightily so, rejecting the possibility of a third way between good and evil. What morality commands, it commands unconditionally.

That is the radical concept put forward by Kant: there are no acceptable excuses; no attenuating or contextual circumstances. When something must be done it must be done; when you *must* do something, you *can* do it. It is always in my power to do what the good requires me to do, and anything that leads me to do otherwise is a false pretext and a lie. In this, it's true that moral law "thwart[s] all our inclinations" and rejects "all the claims of self-love."[5] At the same time, however, it reveals us to ourselves, not with respect to our calculating or egotistical aspects, but precisely in the freedom with which we are able to circumvent our own interests and selfishness. Without the freedom to choose between good and evil, moral law would be a system of pure constraint; without moral law, we would have no way to gauge the power, scope, and force of freedom.

We do not perform a good deed out of benevolence or even love, much less out of sympathy. All of these affects are too fragile and vary according to our moods. Good deeds depend on good will and not from some random emotional state. They represent the capacity to act against oneself and one's ego and independently of its whims and preferences.

You must pass the visibility test, of being in the public eye, in order to overcome the impunity that we all so readily grant ourselves. We must be able to openly proclaim and apply equally to everyone our impulse or motivation to act—what Kant calls the "categorical imperative": "Act as if the maxim of thy action were to become by thy will a universal law of nature."[6]

Is the motive behind my will to action not only aboveboard but appropriate as a principle of action that is applicable to all people? Lies, deceit, envy cannot stand up to the test of absolute transparency and eventual public revelation.

When in the midst of an internal conflict, you must therefore put this imperative Kantian rule into practice: What if everyone acted like me?

Associated Disorder: The Inability to Forgive

While we may sometimes find ourselves on trial, facing the tribunal of our conscience or of moral law, we may also find ourselves in the position of judging the actions of others and of being unable to forgive them. Forgiveness is difficult because it requires us to back down. And if such generosity empowers us, it can also reduce us. We agree to lower ourselves to the level of the person who has offended us and to close the gap that we had sought to open between him and us. Contrarily, a refusal to forgive confers a kind of superiority or inaccessibility—we isolate ourselves way up there in the heights where forgiveness is unthinkable.

But if the error that has been committed were pardonable, it would not require our forgiveness; it would be excusable, at most, or it would cause a rupture and would never be mentioned again. It is the unforgivable that calls for forgiveness. The twentieth-century

French deconstructionist Jacques Derrida put it this way: "[Y]es, there is the unforgivable. Is this not, in truth, the only thing to forgive? The only thing that *calls* for forgiveness? If one is only prepared to forgive what appears forgivable, what the church calls 'venial sin,' then the very idea of forgiveness would disappear."[7]

Some people insist that we can forgive only those who seek forgiveness. But if we forgave only those who asked for it, it would be a calculation of self-interest, or at best a peace treaty, but in no case would it be forgiveness. Forgiveness, according to philosopher and musicologist Vladimir Jankélévitch, is made for "hopeless or incurable cases."[8] It is the cure for incurable suffering.

But if forgiveness is such an extreme, is it really within our power? Do we truly have the capacity to forgive? To pardon and erase errors? Let us agree that that, in nutshell, would be playing God.

FAILURE, DEFEAT, AND BANKRUPTCY

MOST HEALERS ASSERT that we learn with experience, which in this particular case is generally synonymous with failure. It would be therefore by betraying ourselves that we mature. That is as much as to say that there is no such thing as failure—that it is a form of success that has yet to recognize itself for what it is. By that token, there would be no glasses half full or glasses half empty in life, but only the joy of having a glass at all. Whether we fail or whether we succeed, the lessons learned from experience would all be positive in nature.

And we would emerge from our setbacks richer than before; nothing would be wasted, everything would make sense, even our defeats. Sorry to be a killjoy, but philosophy's mission may very well be to insist that a failure is a failure and that a misfortune is not a lesser form of blessing.

The mystique of failure, which amounts to making every defeat an opportunity for apprenticeship and self-improvement, rests on the overvaluation of experience. That in turn can be seen both as a gift and as a miracle—a gift, because it offers insight, and a miracle, because it has the power to turn a negative into a positive. Experience in this context would be a kind of mediator, a transformer of energy, between us and reality; it would negotiate our relations with the real, just as we talk of negotiating a turn in the road. It would be our guide, inspiring and inspired, in our travels along life's roads. And the fact is, we have never been such travelers as we are today—believers, psychoanalysands, and ramblers—we are all on the road, striding onward with confidence. But this is in fact a mystique, or rather a mystification in which all roads lead somewhere, there are no blind alleys or dead ends, and every failure is a partial success. The only thing that counts is the road itself, our road, and the awesome pilgrims that we are in our own bohemian and vagabond lives.

The Placebo of Experience

The truth is, the only thing that experience teaches us is how to fail more elegantly the next time—as Beckett says, "Try again. Fail again. Fail better."[1] And yet we persist in ascribing a pedagogical function to experience, as if we would be unable to learn anything without its instruction. Not "I think, therefore I am" but "I am, therefore I think," as if experience alone allowed me to have any thoughts at all. According to the British philosopher Bertrand Russell, this inductivist *cogito* is a turkey. Newly arrived at the turkey farm, the fowl observes that he is fed every morning at 9 a.m., be it on a Wednesday or a Thursday, be it hot or cold. On the basis of this experience, the turkey draws the following life lesson: "I am always fed at 9 a.m." But on the morning of Christmas Eve, at 9 a.m., he is seized and his throat is cut.

Experience teaches us nothing because life's events are not cumulative, they don't add up to one absolute truth. First, because each experience is unique and incomparable, and thereby incapable of preparing us to face the next. We never live the same experience twice. The only certainties it can offer us are negative ones; it may perhaps help us to learn to recognize faulty thinking (about ourselves, the world, and other people) but not what is true. It is not truth that experience reveals to us but error. It connects us to facts and situations that fly in the face of our predictions. Its power is to "falsify," to refute, and not to verify a hypothesis or a conviction.

The fact is, experience never reflects what we ourselves have invested in it. The only reality we have access to is the one informed by our own beliefs and convictions. A fact has meaning only because we have decided in advance what has and does not have meaning. Experience is therefore never primary but derived, emerging from the way we think and see the world.

We see only what we want to see; it is not what happens to us that shapes us but how we evaluate what happens to us. Experience reveals nothing; we draw from it only that which we believe must be retained. In Kant's formulation, "reason only perceives that which it produces after its own design."[2] It takes the lead, armed with its own judgment and principles, forcing reality to respond to its questions instead of being "content to follow . . . in the leading-strings of nature."[3] And if it happens to learn anything at all from experience, it is not "in the character of a pupil, who listens to all that his master chooses to tell him, but in that of a judge, who compels the witnesses to reply to those questions which he himself thinks fit to propose."[4]

The lessons that our experience and failures allegedly offer teach us only that which we are willing to learn—and which we already knew anyway. If we hope to avoid being a turkey on Christmas Eve, we must stop believing in the so-called power of experience.

BORDERLINE CASES

PHILOSOPHY MUST ALSO be able to address crisis situations, such as identity disorders, madness, suicide, and phobias. Its remedies are not designed exclusively for desperate cases, but it is often by studying pathologies that we begin to understand what constitutes normality. The truth also reveals itself in extreme behaviors, which can often be identified in borderline cases.

That is why reason understands itself only when it also understands madness, why potential suicides may come to embrace clear-eyed hopefulness, and fears and phobias bear witness to the human condition.

Shame and Narcissism

WHO AM I? It is often in the aftermath of failure that we ask ourselves that question. When everything is running smoothly, we're satisfied to go on being who we are and to do what we are doing. The days go by, the weeks slip away without any need to question ourselves. But all it takes is one grain of sand in the mechanism, one tempest, one train wreck to turn us into mysteries to ourselves. Why am I like this? Why do I act like that? And so we find ourselves practicing one of the most classic philosophical activities: introspection. We must practice it like an entomologist, without complacency or concession, without looking for excuses or relying on hackneyed clichés, many of psychoanalytic origin, that are often nothing but the pseudotechnical versions of our innate narcissism.

We must learn to describe ourselves as if we were describing someone else, and hew as closely as possible to reality, even at the risk of behaving shamelessly or shamefully. We must look into every last cranny of ourselves, because it's in the dark corners, broom closets, and other obscure storerooms that we find who we truly are and yet would rather not be. We need to see ourselves naked under stark lighting, with no escape hatch, the way Montaigne did in his *Essays*: "I desire therein to be viewed as I appear in mine own genuine, simple, and ordinary manner, without study and artifice: for it is myself I paint. My defects are therein to be read to the life, and any imperfections and my natural form, so far as public reverence hath permitted me. If I had lived among those nations, which (they say) yet dwell under the sweet liberty of nature's primitive laws, I assure thee I would most willingly have painted myself quite fully and quite naked. Thus, reader, myself am the matter of my book."[1]

You must put yourself to the test, flush yourself out, spy on yourself, dare to say everything you might dare to do, confess your secrets, tell all. "A man must see and study his vice to correct it; they who conceal it from others, commonly conceal it from themselves . . . they withdraw and disguise it from their own consciences."[2] Introspection is butchery—it debones, slices, eviscerates. For the deeper the disorders of our soul, the less we wish to see them, even to the point of being unable to feel them. For Montaigne, the unconscious is a synonym for the lies we tell ourselves about ourselves. "[T]herefore it is that with an unrelenting hand [the diseases of the soul] must often, in full day, be taken to task, opened, and torn from the hollow of the heart."[3] We must seek out whatever we are trying to hide, "even to our inmost and most secret ordures."[4] If we follow this manhunt to the letter, we will find ourselves like the fish in the painting by Chardin or Rembrandt's side of beef—bled, flayed, turned inside out like a glove—so that nothing escapes the blade of introspection.

It is equally important to begin with the physical before plunging rashly into the depths of the psyche, since it is in first dealing uncompromisingly with what can be seen that we are best able to do likewise with what we would prefer not to see. The clinical style used for physical descriptions prepares us to deploy the same style for psychological analysis. In this endeavor, we would do well to turn to the model of François de La Rochefoucauld, a moralist and rebellious nobleman in the court of Louis XIV: "'I am,' says he, 'of a medium height, active, and well-proportioned. My complexion dark, but uniform, a high forehead; and of moderate height, black eyes, small, deep set, eyebrows black and thick but well placed. . . . I have been told I have a little too much chin. I have just looked at myself in the glass to ascertain the fact, and I do not know how to decide. . . . I have in my countenance somewhat of grief and pride, which gives many people an idea I despise them, although I am not at all given to do so. My gestures are very free, rather inclined to be too much so, for in speaking they make me use too much action. Such, candidly, I believe I am in outward appearance, and I believe it will be found that what I have said above of myself is not far from the real case.'"[5]

The one prerequisite for introspection, as we have said, is that it must be uncompromising. It must be like a confession, bringing an unsuspected truth to light. If it is pulled off without upset or discomfort, that is because it is not sincere. If you want to know yourself, you have to cut all the way down to the bone, where flesh, speech, and manners can no longer help you evade and embellish. As the great French writer and ethnographer Michel Leiris put it: "I am disconcerted by an irritating tendency to blush, and by a shiny skin. My hands are thin, rather hairy, the veins distinct; my two middle fingers, curling inward toward the tips, must denote something rather weak or evasive in my character. . . . I loathe unexpectedly catching sight of myself in a mirror, for unless I have prepared myself for the confrontation, I seem humiliatingly ugly to myself each time."[6]

The truth about oneself must have the power both to reveal and to wound, borrowing equally from shame and shamelessness.

MADNESS

Do THE RIGHT-MINDED relegate the mad to the margins of society the way the healthy do to the sick? Do we build walls around hospitals the way we do around prisons, to protect ourselves against deviancy and lock away anything that is off-limits inside a stone dungeon? The French philosopher Michel Foucault seemed to think so. "Is it surprising that prisons resemble factories, schools, barracks, hospitals, which all resemble prisons?"[1] According to Foucault's analysis, all these examples represent an effort to create an architecture of surveillance and behavior control that prevents "close contact, contagions, intimacy, overcrowding, while ensuring aeration and the circulation of air—simultaneously dividing space and leaving it open, ensuring surveillance that is both blanketing and individualizing, even as it carefully isolates those individuals to be surveilled."[2] Religion, medicine, politics, education, and even business impose the same control over individuals, the same domestication and normalization of conduct. Power is a panopticon, able to see all and hear all, including that which is most private and intimate, like the prison conceived by Jeremy Bentham, an English philosopher of the eighteenth century, who served as inspiration to Foucault.[3]

Healthy thinking was in this way to be protected against the contamination of madness, which had to be shut away. It was Descartes who best illustrated this rejection of unreason. It was he who inaugurated the Western era of "the great confinement," which built walls around madness in order to exile and isolate it.[4] But Foucault was wrong on two counts. Far from being uninterested in madness, Descartes was deeply disturbed by it and even characterized so-called normal perception as a kind of truthful hallucination. For it is always the mind, not the eye, that perceives. It is the mind or the brain that decides and determines what is seen, which implies that we can never be sure of having genuine access to reality. Like the madman, the sane person believes that he sees what he sees, and like him he runs the risk of seeing things that do not exist.[5] Perception is thus not very different from hallucination; in both cases, it is the mind that decides what we see, and that can therefore be mistaken.

Foucault's other error is his failure to see how the seventeenth century, which according to him is responsible for this subjugating, policing rationalization, highlighted the similarities between reason and folly, to the point of characterizing all society as a ship of fools, and of seeing the practice of rationality as another form of madness, maladjustment, and abnormality. A sentiment Pascal echoed when he wrote, "Men are so necessarily mad, that not to be mad would amount to another form of madness."[6]

By that token, philosophy is nothing other than the means identified by some to communicate with the madmen that we are. If Plato and Aristotle "wrote on politics, it was as if laying down rules for a lunatic asylum; and if they presented the appearance of speaking of a great matter, it was because they knew that the madmen, to whom they spoke, thought they were kings and emperors. They entered into their principles in order to make their madness as little harmful as possible."[7]

The best use to which we can put our own reason, then, is by learning to survive in the "insane asylum" that is human society.

SOLITUDE AND ISOLATION

INTROSPECTION IS NOT just a risky one-on-one with yourself, without pretense, lies, or excuses. It is a trial by solitude. And that is precisely what can be so scary about solitude—the fact of being alone yet forever in your own company. That is undoubtedly what's behind the perpetual intrusion of background music these days—at restaurants, at the dentist, in dressing rooms—that interminable bass line, often at full volume, never seems to shut up. It's the noise that envelops the silence that surrounds the fact of being yourself, of being with yourself. This coexistence with yourself demands a background drone, a diverting soundtrack that distracts us from that face-to-face encounter with ourselves, that furnishes it and buoys us with its ballast.

We need to feel life and the living surrounding us, mothering us, everywhere and all the time, deflecting the threat of solitude, that confrontation with ourselves. It's almost as if I myself were the greatest source of boredom. And yet, solitude is neither empty nor silent; on the contrary, it is uninterrupted activity. When I am alone, I think. It hardly matters what I think about; I do not go one second without thinking. I am, I exist, I think, fueled by a constant flow of thoughts and ideas, in ongoing conversation with myself.

But it can also happen that I lose touch with myself, when solitude becomes isolation and a loss of all companionship, including my own. Depression, heartbreak, and boredom are just such experiences, when it feels as if I had deserted myself, a solo voice without an interlocutor, me without a partner. I have lost my solitude and am more alone than alone, abandoned by myself. My thoughts, my relations with the world and other people, my self-confidence wither and die.

We stand to lose a great deal by banishing solitude. What we risk in fleeing from ourselves is a loss of freedom. Not the freedom to choose; on the contrary, we are overwhelmed with opportunities to express our preferences, as life and behavior are often about little more than consulting the menu, and the world is a vast market of our desires. *For everlasting love, press 2; for funny and loyal friends, check the box below; if you think Descartes is awesome, "like" him and vote.* . . . We no longer have mere free will—we have become super-wills, perpetually on call to select among options and validate our choices. But is this freedom to roam the supermarket aisles the only kind we possess? Do we not have the capacity to be free in a way that is deeper than mere preference, choice, and clicks?

There must be within us a freedom that is independent of the choices we are offered, a freedom that is able to create its own options, to do more than merely validating or rejecting but to bring something new, unprecedented, unexpected into being.

This freedom is only available in solitude, far from the great bazaar of desires and choices. But, like the French philosopher Henri Bergson, we must deplore the fact that "although we are free whenever we are willing to get back into ourselves, it seldom happens that we are willing."[1]

We therefore need to learn to see solitude as an apprenticeship in freedom and the only means of preserving it.

SUICIDE

WHAT WOULD FREEDOM mean without the opportunity to decide if you wanted to live or die? Without the possibility of suicide? We often find ourselves faced with critical choices—moving to Boston or staying in New York; leaving Marie, changing jobs—but the choice of choices will always be the one confronting our desire for our own death. Determining the value of life requires us to broach the question of suicide. There can be no honest response to the question of whether or not life is worth living unless we give serious consideration to the question of suicide. That, according to Camus, is the "one truly serious philosophical problem."[1]

It is only in imagining suicide that we fully grasp this absurdity of the world and of life, when "[t]he primitive hostility rises up to face us. . . . For a second we cease to understand it. . . . The world evades us because it becomes itself again. That stage scenery masked by habit becomes again what it is. It withdraws at a distance from us. . . . Just one thing: that denseness and that strangeness of the world is the absurd."[2] That absurdity is what we experience when we are depressed and suffering, when the world returns to what it has always been but what we refused to see—a mute and blind world that is deaf and indifferent to our desires.

It is in order to escape that fear and pain that this vision elicits in us that we begin to imagine suicide. As Tolstoy puts it:

"I experienced terror at what awaited me—knew that that terror was even worse than the position I was in; but still I could not patiently await the end. . . . The horror of darkness was too great, and I wished to free myself from it as quickly as possible by noose or bullet. That was the feeling which drew me most strongly towards suicide."[3]

In that sense, paradoxically, consolation and suicide have the same function of putting an end to the pain of suffering, to the infinite pain that we foresee having to endure. There is no suicide on a whim; all suicide is a vision of the future, the perception of a time when misery will endure indefinitely. And it is the impatience to drain this inexhaustible well of sorrow that decides us on suicide. We imagine that the noose or the bullet will end our misery and that, in one way or another, it will bring relief. It is our attraction to that happiness, to its impossible possibility in some way, that guides the act of suicide. As Pascal has it, "All men seek happiness. This is without exception. Whatever different means they employ, they all tend to this end. . . . This is the motive of every action of every man, even of those who hang themselves."[4]

We can also envisage a less extreme and definitive way of securing that "change of scenery," of making a dent in that bleak and monolithic slab of stone that we feel the course of our life to be, by injecting it with something new, some minimal change, as recommended by the ancient Roman orator Cicero: "Sometimes it is desirable to lead one away to new pursuits, solicitudes, cares, occupations. Then too, the cure may often be effected by a change of place, as in the case of invalids who are not convalescent."[5]

Even more effective than a change of place is the courage, as described by Herman Melville, to take to the open water: "Whenever I find myself growing grim about the mouth; whenever it is a damp, drizzly November in my soul . . . then, I account it high time to get to sea as soon as I can. This is my substitute for pistol and ball."[6]

CURIOUS THEORIES

SPORTS MAKE YOU ANTISOCIAL

SPORTS ARE OUR religion. They have their own gods, their own battles, and their own moral law—that of exuberance and pure joy. "I was beside myself . . . I outdid myself!" "That football game? It was brilliant!" We are fanatics for training; *being* is now equivalent to *being in shape*, practically designed, drawn, with crisp contours and sharp edges, the foremost of capital sins being self-neglect, soft flesh, and flabby muscles. A highly ascetic practice, sport commands us to stand up straight and face life with rippling abs and a disciplined cardiovascular system.

The body itself disappears behind the cult dedicated to it. More iron than blood, it becomes quasi-immortal, stripped of anything that might smack of weakness and hence of mortality. The body is no longer alive or, like all living things, subject to decomposition; it has been so worked over, updated, and remodeled that it is almost abstract. We must be wary of this epidemic of hypersport and heed Plato's warning that too much gymnastics makes us antisocial.

The physical discipline we impose on ourselves should contribute to strengthening the soul; our bodily apprenticeship in endurance and fortitude ought to grow into a vigorous aptitude for courage and generosity. But if we make sports an end in itself, if we practice it like a religion, with anathemas and obsessions over purity, it will lead to "hardness and ferocity."[1] We then become the "enemy of philosophy,"[2] having lost all interest in conversation and argument and content with crude, formulaic statements.

Conversely, too much time devoted to art and cultural activities makes a man soft and "in the next stage he begins to melt and waste, until he has wasted away his spirit and cut out the sinews of his soul; and he becomes a feeble warrior." He who does not engage in intellectual exercises is "excitable;—on the least provocation he flames up at once, and is speedily extinguished; instead of having spirit he grows irritable and passionate and is quite impracticable." We must therefore learn to mingle "music with gymnastic," and he who manages to strike a perfect balance between these activities "may be rightly called the true musician and harmonist."[3]

With Plato, illness is always the equivalent of tyranny. It emerges when one tendency or agency—the intellect, the body, or desire—arrogates all power to itself.

We do indeed have a natural tendency to exaggerate, a fascination with extremes, be it extreme deprivation or pleasure: "Certain of the unnecessary pleasures and appetites I conceive to be unlawful; every one appears to have them, but in some persons they are controlled by the laws and by reason."[4]

In politics, this strain of tyranny, this concentration of all power in one place, can be seen above all in democracies. It takes the form of two devastating pathologies: the cult of youth and the cult of cool, where the "the master fears and flatters his scholars, and the scholars despise their masters and tutors; young and old are all alike; and the young man is on a level with the old, and is ready to compete with him in word or deed; and old men condescend to the young and are full of pleasantry and gaiety; they are loth to be thought morose and authoritative, and therefore they adopt the manners of the young."[5] In democracies, sports undoubtedly reinforce such deviance.

GATHERING NO MOSS

THE SO-CALLED WISDOM that comes with age is due more often than not to a newfound inability to be unreasonable. We become admired for what we no longer are: hard-partying, scrappy, reckless, rash. While we have not abandoned our vices, we have agreed to swap them out. And the vices of old age, according to Montaigne, are infinitely worse than those of youth. Growing old is a disease whereby impotence and the desiccation of the body make the spirit bitter and irritable: "I find there more envy, injustice, and malice. Age imprints more wrinkles in the mind than it does on the face; and souls are never, or very rarely seen, that, in growing old, do not smell sour and musty."[1]

In losing our youth, we lose our sense of joy and enthusiasm. We develop, as Montaigne says, a tendency to engage in "impertinent prating," "superstition," "insociable humors" and "foolish and feeble pride."[2] Excessive gaiety gives way to excessive gravity; everything becomes heavier and colder, as if the summer were never return. "I am of late but too reserved, too heavy, and too ripe; years every day read to me lectures of coldness and temperance."[3] Paradoxically, one thing holds true in both old age and youth: the body is the focus of all attention and thought. When we were young, it went looking for whatever trouble it could find;

now that we are old, it rejects trouble of any kind. Which makes life an exercise in endurance and abstinence, "even to stupidity."[4]

"I resist however I am able." That, according to Montaigne, is the only remedy against gathering the moss of old age. In this desiccated phase of life, we must cultivate not only wisdom but impulsiveness, identify every possible off-ramp, find every sort of fork in the road, and choose frivolity over earnestness. "I now and then suffer myself purposely a little to run into disorder, and occupy my mind in wanton and youthful thoughts, wherewith it diverts itself."[5] Lightheartedness, frivolousness, and a little self-indulgence—we fight off old age not with force but with insouciance.

We must also dream, allow our spirit to flower and blossom. We must strive to dispel the sourness of old age by entertaining ourselves with trifles, constantly engaging in games and toys, and replacing envy with delight. "I seize on even the least occasions of pleasure I can meet."[6] We must swap our "dull tranquillity"[7] for an almost greedy vivacity, and cultivate not moderation but appetite.

MAN IS A HUNTING DOG LIKE ANY OTHER

HE HAS BEEN accused of every evil and every disaster; his cold rationalism and sterile idealism have been blamed for nothing less than inducing Western civilization to neglect and scorn the body—Descartes, the undertaker of pleasure and indulgence. The truth is, he was the harbinger of the psychosomatic. For a human being is not pure mind, a *cogito* floating above the surface of the waters, free of the body's constraints. The true human being is the intimate union of body and mind, of the carnal and the spiritual. We are so dependent on the state of health of our organs that, according to Descartes, the job of "making men in most cases wiser and more skilful"[1] belongs more to medicine than to philosophy. We are more than just ideas and concepts; we are fire and passion. The fact that the soul is so closely bound to the body—feeling what it feels, wanting what it wants, loving what it loves—implies that, in one way or another, it is corporeal.

There is a tiny gland beneath the skull that seals the barely conceivable bond between a soul, which does nothing but think, and a body, which is but an "extended substance"[2] (*res extensa*) reduced to occupying space. Known today as the pineal gland, and identified as being responsible for the production of melatonin, which regulates the rhythms of wakefulness and sleep, in Cartesian philosophy this gland ensures communication between two substances—mind and body—that would otherwise be entirely distinct. Descartes, who spent a great deal of time engaged in dissection and anatomical studies, saw it as a kind of communications center. Everything that the body feels, from burning to cold to the jolt of love at first sight, is transmitted to the soul via the pineal gland; in return, the soul translates its sensations into desires and decisions. Body, mind, and brain (where the pineal gland is located) create a circuit in which sensations become representations; then desires; then, finally, action.

The human individual as a whole is a psychosomatic phenomenon. I see a bear (or a beloved); my body begins to tremble; my temperature rises; my throat goes dry; my soul envisions death, love, or destruction; and instructs me either to flee or to fight. The passions—love, fear, courage, or cowardice—are the recoil reaction to what the body is feeling. In romantic passion, the body loves through the soul and the soul desires what the body desires.

But the interesting thing about this entire cycle is that it can be deprogrammed and reprogrammed. You don't overcome a feeling, be it cowardice or love, simply by willing it away. You can't simply decide to stop loving, to stop being afraid, but you can train for it by replacing one inclination, one personality trait, with another. While the sight of John normally makes my body instruct my soul to love him, at any cost, I can associate the sight of that self-same John not with the passion of love but with that of freedom, and pack my bags. Through effort and habit we can learn to alter our response. Fear can be joined not to flight but to courage.

We don't reason with our passions, we recondition them. We change not by an effort of will but by dint of training. We must treat our fervors and desires as a dog trainer would, by substituting one reflex for another. Grand speeches are just as powerless as earnest desire in dealing with our addictions and passions. The only cure lies in our ability to exchange one habit for another.

If an animal can be trained, then we ourselves can certainly learn to master our own passions with the proper training.

GROWING PLANTS AND PERFUME

WHAT A STRANGE sense of guilt we have toward our pleasures, as if it were healthy and natural to slake our thirst and hunger but potentially criminal to seek joy, laughter, or sensuality. Spinoza believed that distrusting our pleasures could lead to bodily and spiritual impotence. Virtue is never fostered by tears, nor does wisdom demand frugality: "I say it is the part of a wise man to refresh and recreate himself with moderate and pleasant food and drink, and also with perfumes, with the soft beauty of growing plants, with dress, with music, with many sports, with theatres, and the like, such as every man may make use of without injury to his neighbour."[1]

Growing plants, jewelry, perfume . . . It's almost like quoting Baudelaire: "Gleaming furniture, polished by years passing, would ornament our bedroom; rarest flowers, their odors vaguely mixed with amber; rich ceilings; deep mirrors; an Oriental splendor— everything there would address our souls, privately, in their sweet native tongue. There, there's only order, beauty: abundant, calm, voluptuous."[2]

Pleasures speak to us in a language that sounds like the language of happiness, of a life in which the body and mind revel in their strength, their respective and combined powers to understand and to act.

Laughter is the perfect example of the kind of unadulterated delight that we are capable of, and that ought to be studied further.

PEDANTRY AND DONKEY'S MILK

WE THINK THE way we eat. In the realm of the intellect, there are gluttons, anorexics, and bulimics; fake gourmets, and real gourmands. Knowledge is like food—it has its virtues and its dangers. The word "educate" has two Latin roots: *educere*, which means "to lead" or "to draw out," and *edere*, meaning "to eat" or "to consume." We must design dietary regimes for the intellect, and above all avoid fats and sugars, which both as foodstuffs and as discourse are either too bland and commonplace, or else too pretentious and falsely sophisticated.

The dietary restrictions that Pascal was compelled to follow for physiological reasons were not so different from those he considers to be critical to a healthy mind, that is, sobriety and freedom of thought. According to his sister, "Amongst his other complaints he had that of not being able to swallow any liquid unless it was heated, nor then unless he did it drop by drop."[1] He also partook of donkey's milk and reviving broths. In the realm of the mind, he insists that anything heavy and cerebral has no real "substance," and that, inversely, that which is light often proves to have the greatest depth.

As Pascal would therefore have it, "To make light of philosophy is to be a true philosopher,"[2] just as irony and laughter are infinitely more subtle than grim earnest. Does not God herself engage in "'bitter irony' and mockery"?[3]

We must learn to live on very little and to make that little our own, trusting only in our own judgment. Not consume everything with gusto, but judiciously assess and winnow. It is wiser to reject and scorn than to approve and pontificate.

One sign of cultivation is the ability to mock culture. It is to have no idols, to think not in terms of yes or no but for oneself. The cultural foodstuffs that we consume usually offer little in the way of nourishment; they make our minds feel more bloated than full.

HAPPINESS IN THE MOMENT IS
THE HAPPINESS OF A COW

THE SECRET OF happiness has been discovered. After centuries of wandering in the wilderness and millennia of frustration, we have finally learned how to be happy. All you need is to learn to live in the moment. To immerse yourself fully, clearly, and unequivocally in the present, here and now. Happiness dwells in the present moment and we never knew it. It does not ask us to give anything up or to take it all in; it resides wholeheartedly in the *here is*: here I am, here is the present, and there is nothing else. The fact is, this present moment that we wish to make our happiness and our home is outside of all time. It is an instant that we would wish to see swell into eternity and suspend the passage of time.

According to Nietzsche, this present happiness, with nothing before or around it, is the happiness of the cow, of the herd: "Consider the cattle, grazing as they pass you by: they do not know what is meant by yesterday or today, they leap about, eat, rest, digest . . . fettered to the moment and its pleasure or displeasure, and thus neither melancholy nor bored."[1] "What happiness!" the cow would say if it could talk. "What happiness!" we say to express our desire to see such happiness go on forever and abolish the course of time.

The happiness by which we would immerse ourselves fully in the present, as if we would never again have any expectations or free will, is the happiness of cattle in the fields—restful, to say the least, but illusory.

For we never live in the present, in the moment. We live as much in the past as we do in the future, or rather, our present is always burdened with both hope and regret, preserving the memory of ancient Edens and probing for a taste of those we hope to see arise.

THE TRANSITIONAL OBJECT

THERE'S NO TAKING life for granted. It's a test that we are forced to undergo right from childhood, and for which it is best to be armed . . . with a blankie. As British psychoanalyst D. W. Winnicott puts it, "the task of reality-acceptance is never completed . . . no human being is free from the strain of relating inner and outer reality, and that relief from this strain is provided by an intermediate area of experience . . . which is not challenged (arts, religion, etc.)."[1] This intermediate area, conceived to make reality more hospitable by every means afforded by culture, is for the adult what play is for children: a welcoming world in which we can be absorbed, and forget and lose ourselves with abandon. Being capable of play, whether our games are those of childhood or adulthood, makes life more livable and reality less hopeless.

Being an adult means having learned to accept reality, which is to say, frustration. According to Winnicott, it is during our young childhood, from zero to four years old, that this negotiation with reality takes place. During this period of transition between the pleasure principle (the ever-ready mother's breast) and the reality principle (the mother as distinct from oneself), the child learns to stop mistaking his desires for reality and to accept that the world does not bend to its will. From all-powerful, he becomes reasonable. But he has an ally in this trial: a "transitional object," usually a blankie—half guardian angel, half stuffed animal—that helps him to endure the frustration linked to the absence of the mother and the revelation that neither the mother nor the world in general answers to his whims.

It is through such toying with absence and presence, the fear that he does not exist in the absence of his mother and his capacity to survive that absence, that the child creates himself. Within that "intermediate area" that we call play, reality, while not yielding to his desires, is not experienced as a threat. We are talking here not about social games, which are always very superficial, but about the capacity to invent, create, imagine, conceive, so as to fill the vacuum and the silence and stave off the fear of collapse.

Thanks to play and the blankie, the child goes from the total dependency of being an infant to the feeling of being a fully distinct individual.

Being an adult means having acquired "the capacity to be alone in the presence of someone"[2] without having to be constantly reassured of one's own existence or having to suffer the indifference of the world, which hears neither our complaints nor our demands. It is nothing less than being capable of inventing a world for oneself, of creating one's own reality.

LEARNING TO UNDERSTAND LOVE
BY WATCHING COMEDIES

PHILOSOPHY CANNOT AVOID taking on the movies, because the most relevant answers to our great questions have been formulated in the studios of Hollywood. According to the American philosopher Stanley Cavell, movies offer the best life lessons and allow us to overcome our doubts and our skepticism about our ability to understand the world, other people, and ourselves. The cinema, which is able to strike a balance between popularity and elitism, is a reservoir of experiences, conversations, solutions, and teachings. It puts life onstage and allows us to unlock its mysteries and clarify its contradictions.

We cannot be the audience for our own life, it's true, but thanks to the movies we can be the privileged witnesses to the lives of others. It is through mainstream comedies and the most highbrow productions alike that we have the possibility of grasping the meaning of our experience and the world that we share with others. Through the movies, we learn to communicate and understand what we undergo and feel. Better yet, the movies make us better people.

That is the meaning of the perfectionism championed by Stanley Cavell. "Perfectionism is the dimension of moral thought directed less to restraining the bad than to releasing the good, as from despair of good (of good and bad in each of us)."[1] Perfectionism promotes an ideal that has not yet been realized but can be, and it is the movies that allow us to see the goodness within us and that give life to it.

If you want proof that existence has a meaning, that happiness is possible, and that love can be rekindled, go to the movies.

More effectively than philosophy—which, contrarily, cultivates defiance and doubt—the movies allow us to reconnect with hope.

ANIMAL PHILOSOPHIES

ON JANUARY 3, 1889, wandering among the streets of Turin, Nietzsche threw himself upon a horse that had been beaten by its coachman, wrapped his arms around the animal, and burst into tears. Folly or philosophy? Definitely philosophy, because it is in our relations with animals, Nietzsche believed, that we find the earliest glimmers of our sense of morality. It is through what we do to animals that we reveal our humanity or inhumanity.[1] It is therefore also for the pain we inflict with impunity upon animals that we cannot be forgiven.

If an animal is not a machine, it may not be treated as such. Nor can it be seen as a mere appendage to ourselves, an appendix with fur or feathers. It is a member of a special partnership that humankind has built over millennia, for at least seventeen thousand years, with the animal kingdom. While we do not speak the same language, we have formed relationships based on service, education, and affection with animals. We are part of a shared social community. There is between us, writes the French agronomist Raphaël Larrère, an "unspoken domestic contract that requires the former not to abuse the latter or to endanger their lives. . . . Animal husbandry consists in assuming responsibility for the protection (from natural enemies and disease), feeding, and reproduction of the domesticated animal. This responsibility imposes obligations on the farmer that correspond to the rights of the animal: the rights to safety, to health, to subsistence, and to reproduction."[2]

Tenderness, emotions, and empathy are inadequate to define or form the basis of our moral relationship to animals. To claim that it is reprehensible to inflict suffering on creatures that are capable of feeling pain and aspiring to happiness[3] reveals the inherent flaw in any moral law based on sentiment. It is limited—because it implies that we would more willingly concern ourselves with mammals than with mosquitoes or earthworms, companion animals than with battery-raised chickens, or even species that are considered to be more beautiful than others—and for that reason its obligations are not unconditional and we will always find waivers and interests to undercut them. Emotions have never been an appropriate basis for building a truly prescriptive moral law that can compel and constrain.

In the seventeenth century, philosophers reconsidered politics and studied its foundations. This led them to develop the hypothesis of a contractual basis for social life, and it was as a function of the nature of that agreement that they formulated the principles of what they believed to be a just political order. In the same vein, it would be appropriate today to draft a social contract between humans and animals that would lay out their reciprocal duties and obligations, as well as rules of civility. That is the only way to guarantee peace and dignity, both for humans and for animals is neither by combining nor by pitting the two kingdoms against one another that we will succeed in raising the moral standing of humankind, for "It is dangerous to make man see too clearly his equality with the brutes without showing him his greatness. It is also dangerous to make him see his greatness too clearly, apart from his vileness. It is still more dangerous to leave him in ignorance of both. But it is very advantageous to show him both."[4]

ACKNOWLEDGMENTS

I thank my editor, Monique Labrune, without whom I could not have brought this project to fruition, for as La Fontaine writes, "be he monkey or a writer of books, the worst of all species is the author." Thanks, too, to Melinda Fiant for her patience. I thank the friends who listened to me, supported me, reread me, corrected me, and occasionally even agreed with me; even if their names have been changed, they will be able to recognize themselves in each of the preceding chapters. I thank my F, my BS, my N, and PG, who are always with me.

NOTES

Epigraph

1. Blaise Pascal, *Pensées*, 331, eBooks@Adelaide, University of Adelaide, 2014.

Introduction: It's Not All Fun and Games

1. John Donne, "The Litanie," xxvii, *The Poems of John Donne, Edited from the Old Editions and Numerous Manuscripts*, 2 vols., ed. Herbert J. C. Grierson (Oxford: Clarendon Press, 1912), https://www.gutenberg.org/files/48688/48688-h/48688-h.htm.

2. Porphyry, *Letter to Marcella, His Wife*, trans. Alice Zimmern (London: Priory Press, 1910), 31, http://www.tertullian.org/fathers/porphyry_marcella_03_revised_text.htm.

Use as Directed: Healing Your Life

1. Sören Kierkegaard, *The Sickness Unto Death*, Walter Lowerie trans., Princeton University Press (Princeton, NJ, 1941), preface.

2. Plato, *Alcibiades I*, trans. Benjamin Jowett, https://www.gutenberg.org/files/1676/1676-h/1676-h.htm.

3. Saint Augustine, book X, *The Confessions of Saint Augustine*, trans. Edward Bouverie Pusey, https://www.sacred-texts.com/chr/augconf/aug10.htm.

4. Saint Augustine, book IV, *The Confessions of Saint Augustine*, https://www.sacred-texts.com/chr/augconf/aug04.htm.

5. Plato, *Gorgias*, in *Plato in Twelve Volumes*, vol. 3, *Lysis. Symposium. Gorgias*, trans. W. R. M. Lamb (1914; repr., Cambridge, MA, Harvard University Press; London: William Heinemann, 1967), 500d.

6. René Descartes, "Part III," *Discourse on Method* in *Discourse on Method and Meditations of First Philosophy*, trans. Elizabeth S. Haldane (Digireads.com, 2016), 30.

7. Maurice Merleau-Ponty, *Sense and Non-Sense*, trans. Hubert L. Dreyfus and Patricia Allen Dreyfus (Evanston, IL: Northwestern University Press, 1964), 38.

8. Plato, *Gorgias*, 521e.

9. Plato, *Plato in Twelve Volumes*, vol. 6, *Republic*, vol. II, book VII, trans. Paul Shorey (London: Heinemann, 1935), 515a.

10. As quoted by Eric Sellin, *The Dramatic Concepts of Antonin Artaud* (1968; repr., New Orleans, LA: Quid Pro Books, 2017), 67.

11. Antonin Artaud, Letter to Jean Paulhan, January 25, 1936.

12. Antonin Artaud, "The Theater and the Plague," in *The Theater and Its Double*, trans. Mary Caroline Richards (New York: Grove Press, 1958), 31–32.

13. Ibid., 46.

14. Artaud, "The Theater of Cruelty (Second Manifesto)," in *The Theater and Its Double*, 122–23.

15. Georges Canguilhem, *Études d'histoire et de philosophie des sciences: concernant les vivants et al vie* (Paris: Librairie Philosophique J. Vrin, 1994), 366; translated here by Jesse Browner.

AFFLICTIONS OF THE BODY

Beautiful, Fat, Ugly, and Skinny

1. Except, perhaps, Montaigne in his *Essays*.

2. Plato, *Parmenides*, in *Plato in Twelve Volumes*, vol. 4, *Cratylus, Parmenides, Greater Hippias, Lesser Hippias*, trans. Harold North Fowler (London: Heinemann, 1970), 130c–d.

3. Emmanuel Levinas, *Ethics and Infinity: Conversations with Philippe Nemo*, trans. Richard A. Cohen (Pittsburgh: Duquesne University Press, 1995).

4. Jacques Derrida, *The Animal That Therefore I Am*, trans. David Wills (New York: Fordham University Press, 2008), 3–4.

The Last Act Is Tragic

1. Michel de Montaigne, "Of Friendship," *Essays of Michel de Montaigne*, ed. William Carew Hazlitt, trans. Charles Cotton, https://www.gutenberg.org/files/3600/3600-h/3600-h.htm.

2. Epicurus, *Letter to Menoeceus*, trans. Robert Drew Hicks, http://classics.mit.edu/Epicurus/menoec.html.

3. Horace, "Carpe Diem," *The Odes*, book I, ode XI, trans. A. S. Kline, Poetry in Translation, https://www.poetryintranslation.com/PITBR/Latin/HoraceOdesBkI.php#anchor_Toc39402008.

4. Albert Camus, "The Wind at Djemila," in *Lyrical and Critical Essays*, ed. Philip Thody, trans. Ellen Conroy Kennedy (1968; repr., New York: Vintage, 1970), 77.

5. Blaise Pascal, fragment 210, Section III, "Of the Necessity of the Wager," *Pascal's Thoughts*, in *Thoughts, Letters and Minor Works*, trans. W. F. Trotter (*Thoughts*), M. L. Booth (*Letters*), and O. W. Wight (*Minor Works*), Harvard Classics 48, ed. Charles William Eliot (New York: P. F. Collier, 1910), 79, https://ia800708.us.archive.org/20/items/Harvard-Classics/048_Harvard_Classics.pdf.

6. Michel de Montaigne, *Essays*, "Of Diversion."

7. Ibid.

Nothing Is More Despicable Than Illness

1. Albert Camus, "The Wind at Djemila," in *Lyrical and Critical Essays*, ed. Philip Thody, trans. Ellen Conroy Kennedy (1968; repr., New York: Vintage, 1970), 77.

2. A phrase coined by the surgeon René Leriche, as quoted by Canguilhem, according to whom health, in this context, is the subject's "state of unawareness where the subject and his body are one. Conversely, the awareness of the body consists in a feeling of limits, threats, obstacles to health." Georges Canguilhem, *The Normal and the Pathological*, trans. Carolyn R. Fawcett with Robert S. Cohen (New York: Zone Books, 1991), 91.

3. Jean-Marie Guyau, *A Sketch of Morality Independent of Obligation or Sanction*, trans. Gertrude Kapteyn (1898; repr., London: Forgotten Books, 2012), 23–24.

4. Ivan Illich, *Limits to Medicine: Medical Nemesis; The Expropriation of Health* (London: Marion Boyers Publishers, 2010), 3.

5. Aristotle, *Rhetoric*, 1406B.

6. Susan Sontag, *Illness as Metaphor* (New York: Farrar, Straus and Giroux, 1978), 3.

7. Ibid., 3.

Suffering

1. René Descartes, "Meditation VI: Of the Existence of Material Things, and of the real distinction between the Soul and Body of Man," in *Discourse on Method and Meditations of First Philosophy*, trans. Elizabeth S. Haldane (Digireads.com, 2016), 110.

2. Jan Patočka, *Heretical Essays in the Philosophy of History*, ed. James Dodd, trans. Erazim Kohák (Peru, IL: Open Court, 1996), 134.

3. Paul Ricoeur, *"La souffrance n'est pas la douleur"* (Suffering is not pain), *Psychiatrie française* 1992. Vol. 23, May 1992, 9–18.

Aging

1. Pierre de Ronsard, *Derniers vers*. Editions la Bibliothèque Digitale.

2. Ibid.

3. Simone de Beauvoir, *The Force of Circumstance*, trans. Richard Howard (New York: Putnam, 1965), 672.

4. Simone de Beauvoir, *The Coming of Age*, trans. Patrick O'Brian (1972; repr., New York: W. W. Norton, 1996), 539–40.

5. Maurice Merleau-Ponty, *Sense and Non-Sense*, trans. Hubert L. Dreyfus and Patricia Allen Dreyfus (Evanston, IL: Northwestern University Press, 1964), 38.

6. Ibid., 40.

7. Hannah Arendt, *The Human Condition* (Chicago: University of Chicago Press, 1958), 243–46.

8. Ibid.

Tobacco, Alcohol, and Addiction

1. Jean Esquirol, "Lypemania or Melancholy," in *Mental Maladies: A Treatise on Insanity*, trans. E. K. Hunt (Philadelphia: Lea and Blanchard, 1845).

2. Jean Racine, *Phaedra*, II. v, trans. A. S. Kline, Poetry in Translation, https://www.poetryintranslation.com/klineasphaedra.php.

3. See the analysis of Antonio R. Damasio in *Descartes' Error: Emotion, Reason, and the Human Brain* (1994; repr., New York: Penguin, 2005).

4. Aristotle, *Nichomachaen Ethics*, II.6, trans. David Ross (Oxford: Oxford University Press, 2009), http://classics.mit,edu/Aristotle/nicomachaen.2.ii.html.

5. William Shakespeare, *King Lear*, II.iv.

6. Seneca, *On Anger*, I.9, http://www.sophia-project.org/uploads/1/3/9/5/13955288/seneca_anger.pdf.

7. Ibid., II.3.

8. Seneca, *Letters to Lucilius*, 116, https://en.wikisource.org/wiki/Moral_letters_to_Lucilius/Letter_116.

9. Ibid.

Hunger: The Dietetics of Pleasure

1. Arthur Schopenhauer, *The World as Will and Representation*, trans. and ed. Judith Norman, Alistair Welchman, and Christopher Janaway (Cambridge: Cambridge University Press, 2014), 219–20.

2. Étienne de La Boétie, *Discourse on Voluntary Servitude*, trans. Harry Kurz (Indianapolis: Hackett, 1942), https://oll.libertyfund.org/titles/boetie-the-discourse-of -voluntary-servitude.

3. Plato, *Gorgias*, in *Plato in Twelve Volumes*, vol. 3, *Lysis. Symposium. Gorgias*, trans. W. R. M. Lamb (1914; repr., Cambridge, MA, Harvard University Press; London: William Heinemann, 1967), 492c, 494c, http://www.perseus.tufts .edu/hopper/text?doc=Perseus%3Atext%3A1999.01.0178%3Atext%3DGorg .%3Asection%3D494c.

4. Arthur Schopenhauer, section 9, in *Counsels and Maxims*, trans. T. Bailey Saunders, https://www.gutenberg.org/files/10715/10715-h/10715-h.htm#link2H_4 _0008.

5. Baruch Spinoza, part IV, note to corollary II of proposition XLV, in *Ethics*, trans. R. H. M. Elwes, https://www.gutenberg.org/files/3800/3800-h/3800-h .htm#chap04.

6. Albert Camus, "Nuptials at Tipasa," in *Lyrical and Critical Essays*, ed. Philip Thody, trans. Ellen Conroy Kennedy (1968; repr., New York: Vintage, 1970), 67.

7. Albert Camus, "The Almond Trees," in *Lyrical and Critical Essays*, 137.

8. Albert Camus, "The Sea Close By," in *Lyrical and Critical Essays*, 181.

Afflictions of the Brain

1. Avital Ronell, *Stupidity* (Champaign: University of Illinois Press, 2002), 44.

2. Plato, *The Republic*, book VII, trans. Benjamin Jowett, http://classics.mit.edu/ Plato/republic.8.vii.html.

3. Immanuel Kant: "[A] full and clear definition ought, in philosophy, rather to form the conclusion than the commencement of our labours." *Critique of Pure Reason*, trans. J. M. D. Meiklejohn (CreateSpace Independent Publishing Platform, 2014), 365.

4. René Descartes, *Discourse on Method and Meditations of First Philosophy*, trans. Elizabeth S. Haldane (Digireads.com, 2016), 14.

AFFLICTIONS OF THE SOUL

1. Plato, "Philebus," trans. Benjamin Jowett, https://sacred-texts.com/cla/plato /philebus.htm.

2. Maurice Merleau-Ponty, *Phenomenology of Perception*, trans. Donald Landes (Abingdon, UK: Routledge, 2012), 195.

Living

1. On the idea of DYI, see Claude Lévi-Strauss, *The Savage Mind* (Chicago: University of Chicago Press, 1966).

2. Life asks us to wager, to choose who we want to be: "Yes; but you must wager. It is not optional. You are embarked. Which will you choose then? Let us see. Since you must choose, let us see which interests you least." Blaise Pascal, "Of the Necessity of the Wager," Section III of *Pascal's Thoughts*, in *Thoughts, Letters and Minor Works*, trans. W. F. Trotter (*Thoughts*), M. L. Booth (*Letters*), and O. W. Wight (*Minor Works*), Harvard Classics 48, ed. Charles William Eliot (New York: P. F. Collier, 1910), 85, https://ia800708.us.archive.org/20/items/Harvard-Classics/048_Harvard_Classics.pdf.

3. Jean-Paul Sartre, *Existentialism Is a Humanism* (1996; repr., New Haven, CT: Yale University Press, 2007), 37. Sartre goes on to critique this position.

4. Ibid., 38.

5. Gottfried Wilhelm Leibniz, *Sämtliche Schriften und Briefe*, vol. VI, 3, (Berlin: Akademie-Ausgabe, 1981), 378.

Daily Life

1. Michel de Montaigne, "Of Vanity," in *Essays of Michel de Montaigne*, ed. William Carew Hazlitt, trans. Charles Cotton, https://www.gutenberg.org/files/3600/3600-h/3600-h.htm.

2. Maurice Blondel, *Action*, trans. Oliva Blanchette (1893; repr., Notre Dame, IN: University of Notre Dame Press, 1984), 5.

3. "No man is a hero to his valet, but not because that man is not a hero, but rather because the latter is—a valet, a person with whom the hero deals not as a hero but as someone who eats, drinks, gets dressed, in general in the singularity of the hero's needs and ideas." Georg Wilhelm Friedrich Hegel, *The Phenomenology of Spirit*, trans. and ed. Terry Pinkard (1807; repr., Cambridge: Cambridge University Press, 2018), 385.

4. Raymond Queneau, *Zazie* (*Zazie dans le métro*), trans. Barbara Wright (London: John Calder, 1982), 100.

5. Marcel Proust, *Time Regained*, trans. Stephen Hudson, https://ebooks.adelaide.edu.au/p/proust/marcel/p96t/complete.html.

6. Friedrich Nietzsche, *The Gay Science*, ed. Bernard Williams, trans. Josefine Nauck-hoff (Cambridge: Cambridge University Press, 2012), 167.

7. Ibid., 168.

Akrasia, or the Counterfeit Disease

1. Saint Augustine, book VIII, in *The Confessions of Saint Augustine*, trans. Edward Bouverie Pusey, https://www.sacred-texts.com/chr/augconf/aug08.htm.

2. Saint Augustine, "Did I wish, if only by gesture, to rebel against thy law, even though I had no power to do so actually—so that, even as a captive, I might produce a sort of counterfeit liberty . . .", book II, *Confessions*, in *Confessions and Enchiridion*, trans. and ed. Albert C. Outler (Philadelphia: Westminster Press, 1955), 57.

3. Plato, book I, *Laws*, trans. Benjamin Jowett, http://classics.mit.edu/Plato/laws.1.i.html.

4. Pierre Corneille, *The Cid*, III.iv, Poetry in Translation, https://www.poetryintrans-lation.com/PITBR/French/LeCidActIII.php#anchor_Toc168900825.

5. Pierre Corneille, *Médée*, I.v, trans. Jesse Browner.

6. See Jon Elster, *Le Laboureur et ses enfants* (Paris: Minuit, 1986), 101.

7. Blaise Pascal, fragment 252, Section IV, "Of the Means of Belief," *Thoughts*, in *Thoughts, Letters and Minor Works*, trans. W. F. Trotter (*Thoughts*), M. L. Booth (*Letters*), and O. W. Wight (*Minor Works*), Harvard Classics 48, ed. Charles William Eliot (New York: P. F. Collier, 1910), 93, https://ia800708.us.archive.org/20/items/Harvard-Classics/048_Harvard_Classics.pdf.

Burnout

1. Friedrich Nietzsche, *Human, All Too Human*, trans. Helen Zimmern (Digireads.com Publishing, 2018), 149.

2. Karl Marx, "First Manuscript," in *Economic & Philosophic Manuscripts of 1844*, trans. Martin Milligan, 30, https://www.marxists.org/archive/marx/works/download/pdf/Economic-Philosophic-Manuscripts-1844.pdf.

3. Karl Marx, *Capital*, vol. II, 138, https://www.marxists.org/archive/marx/works/download/doc/Capital-Volume-II.doc.

4. Karl Marx and Friedrich Engels, "Private Property and Communism," in *A Critique of the German Ideology*, 13, https://www.marxists.org/archive/marx/works/download/Marx_The_German_Ideology.pdf.

5. "[T]he communist revolution is directed against the preceding mode of activity, does away with labour," in "Contradictions of Big Industry: Revolution," ibid.

6. Friedrich Nietzsche, *The Gay Science*, ed. Bernard Williams, trans. Josefine Nauckhoff (Cambridge: Cambridge University Press, 2012), 43–44.

Good Company, Bad Company: "Man Is Wolf to Man"

1. In his dedication to *De Cive*, Thomas Hobbes borrows the phrase from the Roman playwright Plautus.

2. Friedrich Engels, "The English Constitution," *Vorwärts!* no. 75, September 18, 1844, https://marxists.catbull.com/archive/marx/works/1844/condition-england/ch02.htm.

3. Thomas Hobbes, "Out of Civil States," *Leviathan* (1651), http://www.gutenberg.org/files/3207/3207-h/3207-h.htm.

Fear and Trembling

1. Sigmund Freud, "12. Determinism—Chance—and Superstitious Beliefs Points of View," in *Psychopathology of Everyday Life*, trans A. A. Brill (1914), http://www.reasoned.org/dir/lit/PEL_freud.pdf.

2. Ibid.

3. Baruch Spinoza, prop LIX, in *The Ethics*, trans. R. H. M. Elwes, http://www.gutenberg.org/files/3800/3800-h/3800-h.htm.

4. Baruch Spinoza, Preface, *A Theological-Political Treatise*, trans. R. H. M. Elwes, http://www.gutenberg.org/files/989/898-h/989-h.htm#preface.

5. Ibid.

6. Ibid.

7. Ibid.

8. Baruch Spinoza, prop LXVII, in *The Ethics* (1677), trans. R. H. M. Elwes, https://www.gutenberg.org/files/3800/3800-h/3800-h.htm.

Love

1. Julien Hayneufve, *L'Ordre de la vie et des moeurs* (1639), t. I, p. 325; "*L'amour est l'unique passion qui nous agite,*" Jean-François Senault, *De l'usage des passions* (1641), 27.

2. Immanuel Kant, *Anthropology from a Pragmatic Point of View*, trans. Mary J. Gregor (The Hague: Martinus Nijhoff, 1974), 133.

3. Immanuel Kant, *Lectures on Ethics*, eds. Peter Heath and J. B. Schneewind, trans. Peter Heath (Cambridge: Cambridge University Press, 1997), 155.

4. Ibid.

5. Jean de la Fontaine, "The Two Pigeons," in *Fables*, trans. Sir Edward Marsh (New York: Alfred A. Knopf, 2001), 148.

6. Lucretius, *De rerum natura* (*On the Nature of Things*), IV, trans. William Ellery Leonard, http://classics.mit.edu/Carus/nature_things.4.iv.html.

7. Ibid.

8. Ibid.

9. Ibid.

10. Ibid.

Love at First Sight

1. Marcel Proust, *Swann in Love*, trans. Brian Nelson (Oxford: Oxford University Press, 2017), 181.

Opium Smokers

1. Karl Marx, *Introduction to "A Contribution to the Critique of Hegel's Philosophy of Right,"* in Karl Marx and Friedrich Engels, *Collected Works*, vol. 3 (New York: International Publishers, 1975), 176.

2. Karl Marx and Friedrich Engels, Preface to *The German Ideology*, trans. Cyril Smith, 2002, based on work done jointly with Don Cuckson, https://www.marxists.org/archive/marx/works/1845/german-ideology/preface.htm.

3. Ibid., "Part I: Feuerbach—Proletarians and Communism—Individual, Class, and Community," https://www.marxists.org/archive/marx/works/1845/german-ideology/ch01d.htm.

4. Hans Blumenberg, "An Anthropological Approach to the Contemporary Significance of Rhetoric," in *After Philosophy: End or Transformation?*, eds. Kenneth Baynes, James Bohman, and Thomas McCarthy, trans. Robert M. Wallace (Cambridge, MA: MIT Press, 1987), 439.

5. Hans Blumenberg, "The Name Breaks into the Chaos of the Unnamed," in *Work on Myth*, trans. Robert M. Wallace (Cambridge, MA: MIT Press, 1985), 35.

6. Ibid., 34.

7. Hans Blumenberg, "An Anthropological Approach to the Contemporary Significance of Rhetoric," 438–39.

Regrets and Remorse

1. Charles Baudelaire, "The Irreparable," in *The Flowers of Evil*, trans. James McGowan (Oxford: Oxford University Press, 1998), 111.

2. Michel de Montaigne, "Of Experience," in *Essays of Michel de Montaigne*, ed. William Carew Hazlitt, trans. Charles Cotton, https://www.gutenberg.org/files/3600/3600-h/3600-h.htm.

3. Ibid.

4. Ibid.

5. Ibid.

THE WORRIES OF EVERYDAY LIFE

Money

1. Karl Marx, "The Power of Money," in *Economic and Philosophic Manuscripts of 1844*, trans. Martin Milligan, https://marxists.catbull.com/archive/marx/works/1844/manuscripts/power.htm.

2. Immanuel Kant, *Critique of Pure Reason*, trans. J. M. D. Meiklejohn (CreateSpace Independent Publishing Platform, 2014), 314.

3. Ibid., 315.

4. That is the reasoning behind Hegel's critique of Kant in his *Lectures on the Proofs of the Existence of God*. Marx, for his part, demonstrates that money is of the same nature as the existence of God, that is, a social representation, a belief: "Real thalers have the same existence that the imagined gods have," "Critique of Plutarch's Polemic against the Theology of Epicurus," in *The Difference Between the Democritean and Epicurean Philosophy of Nature*, https://archive.org/stream/Marx_Karl_-_Doctoral_Thesis_-_The_Difference_Between_the_Democritean_and_Epicure/Marx_Karl__Doctoral_Thesis__The_Difference_Between_the_Democritean_and_Epicurean_Philosophy_of_Nature_djvu.txt. That is how "all humanity has incurred *debts on its gods*." What is salvation if not a way of going into business with the gods, of monetizing your own redemption?

Neighborhood Problems

1. Immanuel Kant, "Idea for a Universal History from a Cosmopolitan Point of View," Fourth Thesis, in *On History*, trans. Lewis White Beck (Indianapolis, IN: Bobbs-Merrill, 1963), https://www.marxists.org/reference/subject/ethics/kant/universal-history.htm.

2. Ibid.

3. Arthur Schopenhauer, "Our Relation to Ourselves," in *Counsels and Maxims*, trans. T. Bailey Saunders, https://www.gutenberg.org/files/10715/10715-h/10715-h.htm#link2H_4_0008.

4. Arthur Schopenhauer, "Similes, Parables and Fables," in *Parerga and Paralipomena*, vol. 2, trans. and ed. Adrian Del Caro and Christopher Janaway (Cambridge: Cambridge University Press, 2015), 584.

The Bore, the Pygmalion, and the Soliloquist

1. Thomas Aquinas, *The Summa Theologica*, Ia, IIae, q. 40 ("All foolish . . . persons attempt everything.").

2. Michel de Montaigne, "On the Art of Conversation," in *The Complete Essays*, trans. and ed. M. A. Screech (London: Penguin Books, 1987), 1045.

3. E. M. Cioran, *A Short History of Decay*, trans. Richard Howard (New York: Arcade Publishing, 2012), 17.

4. Ibid.

5. Ibid.

6. Arthur Schopenhauer, "Our Relation to Ourselves," in *Counsels and Maxims*, trans. T. Bailey Saunders, https://www.gutenberg.org/files/10715/10715-h/10715-h .htm#link2H_4_0008.

7. Michel de Montaigne, "Of the Art of Conference," in *Essays of Michel de Montaigne*, ed. William Carew Hazlitt, trans. Charles Cotton, https://www.gutenberg.org /files/3600/3600-h/3600-h.htm.

8. Ibid.

9. Ibid.

10. Ibid.

(Other People's) Children, Friends, and Family

1. René Descartes, letter to Marin Mersenne, AT VIII, 110–111.

2. Michel de Montaigne, "Of the Art of Conference," in *Essays of Michel de Montaigne*, ed. William Carew Hazlitt, trans. Charles Cotton, https://www.gutenberg.org /files/3600/3600-h/3600-h.htm.

3. Plato, book V, *Republic*, trans. Benjamin Jowett, http://classics.mit.edu/Plato /republic.6.v.html.

4. Ibid., book II, http://classics.mit.edu/Plato/republic.3.ii.html.

5. Ibid., book V, http://classics.mit.edu/Plato/republic.6.v.html.

Bosses and Colleagues.

1. Étienne de La Boétie, *Discourse on Voluntary Servitude*, trans. Harry Kurz (Auburn, AL: Ludwig von Mises Institute, 1975), 72.

2. Ibid., 73.

3. Ibid., 79.

4. Paul Lafargue, *The Right to be Lazy*, trans. Charles H. Kerr (CreateSpace Independent Publishing Platform, 2016), 10.

5. Ibid., 28.

6. Henri Laborit, *Éloge de la fuite* (*In Praise of Escape*), (Paris: Gallimard, 1985); trans. here by Jesse Browner.

7. Blaise Pascal, fragment 336, section V, "Justice and the Reason of Effects," in *Thoughts, Letters and Minor Works*, trans. W. F. Trotter (*Thoughts*), M. L. Booth (*Letters*), and O. W. Wight (*Minor Works*), Harvard Classics 48, ed. Charles William Eliot (New York: P. F. Collier, 1910), 116, https://ia800708.us.archive.org/20/items/Harvard-Classics/048_Harvard_Classics.pdf.

8. Blaise Pascal, "On the Condition of the Great," *Minor Works*, 381.

9. Blaise Pascal, fragment 320, section V, "Justice and the Reason of Effects," *Thoughts*, 111.

Getting Wet at the Pool, and Other Things You Can't Change

1. Epictetus, section 4, *The Enchiridion*, trans. Elizabeth Carter, http://classics.mit.edu/Epictetus/epicench.html.

2. Ibid., section 2.

3. Ibid., section 15.

4. Ibid., section 17.

5. Ibid.

MENTAL DISORDERS, TEMPORARY AND CHRONIC

Depression, Melancholy, Taedium Vitae, or Acedia

1. Seneca, *Of Peace of Mind*, Section II, trans. Aubrey Stewart (Los Angeles: Enhanced Media, 2016), 11.

2. Charles Baudelaire, "Spleen," in *The Flowers of Evil*, trans. Lewis Piaget Shanks (New York: Ives Washburn, 1931).

3. Ibid.

4. Evagrius Ponticus, *Praktikos*, trans. Luke Dysinger, http://evagriusponticus.net/cpg2430.html.

5. Saint Nilus, chapter XIV, *De octo spiritibus malitiae*.

Jealousy, Envy, and Schadenfreude

1. Sigmund Freud, *Civilization and its Discontents*, trans. James Strachey (W. W. Norton, 2010), 65.

2. Norbert Elias, *The Civilizing Process*, trans. Edmund Jephcott (Oxford: Blackwell, 2000), 157.

LIFE'S LITTLE ACCIDENTS

Mistakes, Sins, and a Guilty Conscience

1. Immanuel Kant, *The Metaphysics of Morals*, trans. and ed. Mary Gregor (Cambridge: Cambridge University Press, 2017), 203.

2. Ibid.

3. Plato, *Plato in Twelve Volumes*, vol. 3, *Lysis. Symposium. Gorgias*, trans. W. R. M. Lamb (1914; Cambridge, MA, Harvard University Press; London: William Heinemann, 1967).

4. Plato, book II, *Republic*, trans. Benjamin Jowett, http://classics.mit.edu/Plato/republic.3.ii.html.

5. Immanuel Kant, *Critique of Practical Reason*, trans. Mary Gregor (Cambridge: Cambridge University Press, 2015), 61–63.

6. Immanuel Kant, *Fundamental Principles of the Metaphysic of Morals*, trans. Thomas Kingsmill Abbot, https://www.gutenberg.org/files/5682/5682-h/5682-h.htm.

7. Jacques Derrida, *On Cosmopolitanism and Forgiveness*, trans. Mark Dooley and Michael Hughes (Abingdon, UK: Routledge, 2001), 32.

8. Vladimir Jankélévitch, *Forgiveness*, trans. Andrew Kelley (Chicago: University of Chicago Press, 2005), 156.

Failure, Defeat, and Bankruptcy

1. Samuel Beckett, "Worstward Ho," in *Nohow On* (New York: Grove Press, 2014), 89.

2. Immanuel Kant, Preface to the Second Edition, *Critique of Pure Reason*, trans. J. M. D. Meiklejohn (CreateSpace Independent Publishing Platform, 2014), xxvii.

3. Ibid.

4. Ibid.

BORDERLINE CASES

Identity Disorders: Shame and Narcissism

1. Michel de Montaigne, "The Author to the Reader," in *Essays of Michel de Montaigne*, ed. William Carew Hazlitt, trans. Charles Cotton, https://www.gutenberg.org/files/3600/3600-h/3600-h.htm.

2. Ibid., "Upon Some Verses of Virgil."

3. Ibid.

4. Ibid.

5. François de La Rochefoucauld, translator's introduction, *Reflections; or Sentences and Moral Maxims*, trans. J. W. Willis Bund and J. Hain Friswell (London: Simpson Low, Son, and Marston, 1871), https://www.gutenberg.org/files/9105/9105-h/9105-h.htm.

6. Michel Leiris, *Manhood: A Journey from Childhood into the Fierce Order of Virility*, trans. Richard Howard (Chicago: University of Chicago Press, Chicago, 1992), 3–4.

Madness

1. Michel Foucault, *Discipline & Punish: The Birth of the Prison*, trans. Alan Sheridan (New York: Vintage Books, 1995), 228.

2. Michel Foucault, "*L'oeil du pouvoir*" (*The Eye of Power*), interview with J.-P. Barou and M. Perrot, in Jeremy Bentham, *Le Panoptique* (Paris: Belfond, 1977), 9–31; trans. here by Jesse Browner.

3. Jeremy Bentham, *The Works of Jeremy Bentham*, vol. IV, *Panopticon* (Edinburgh: William Tait, 1843), 84–85.

4. Michel Foucault, *Madness and Civilization: A History of Insanity in the Age of Reason*, trans. Richard Howard (1965; repr., New York: Vintage Books, 1988), 38 *et seq.*

5. René Descartes, *La Dioptrique*, AT VI, 141. I thank Emanuela Scribano for having clarified this point in *Macchine con la mente. Fisiologia e metafisica tra Cartesio et Spinoza* (Rome: Carocci editore, 2015), 13–75.

6. Blaise Pascal, fragment 414, section VI, "The Philosophers," *Pascal's Thoughts*, in *Thoughts, Letters and Minor Works*, trans. W. F. Trotter (*Thoughts*), M. L. Booth (*Letters*), and O. W. Wight (*Minor Works*), Harvard Classics 48, ed. Charles William Eliot (New York: P. F. Collier, 1910), 133, https://ia800708.us.archive.org/20/items/Harvard-Classics/048_Harvard_Classics.pdf.

7. Blaise Pascal, fragment 331, "Justice and the Reason of Effects," 331.

Solitude and Isolation

1. Henri Bergson, *Time and Free Will: An Essay on the Immediate Data of Conscious-ness*," trans. F. L. Pogson (1910; repr., London: George Allen & Unwin, 1950), 130.

Suicide

1. Albert Camus, *The Myth of Sisyphus*, trans. Justin O'Brien (New York: Alfred A. Knopf, 1955), 3.

2. Ibid., 14.

3. Leo Tolstoy, *A Confession*, trans. Aylmer Maude (Mineola, NY: Dover Publications, 2005), 20.

4. Blaise Pascal, fragment 425, section VI, "The Philosophers," in *Pascal's Thoughts*, in *Thoughts, Letters and Minor Works*, trans. W. F. Trotter (*Thoughts*), M. L. Booth (*Letters*), and O. W. Wight (*Minor Works*), Harvard Classics 48, ed. Charles William Eliot (New York: P. F. Collier, 1910), 134, https://ia80708.us.archive.org/20/items/Harvard-Classics/048_Harvard_Classics.pdf.

5. Marcus Tullius Cicero, *Tusculan Disputations*, trans. Andrew P. Peabody (Boston: Little, Brown, 1886), 244.

6. Herman Melville, *Moby-Dick* (1851; repr., London: Macmillan, 2016), 31.

CURIOUS THEORIES

Too Much Sport Makes You Antisocial

1. Plato, book III, *Republic*, trans. Benjamin Jowett, http://classics.mit.edu/Plato/republic.4.iii.html.

2. Ibid., book V, http://classics.mit.edu/Plato/republic.6.v.html.

3. Ibid, book III, http://classics.mit.edu/Plato/republic.4.iii.html.

4. Ibid., book IX, http://classics.mit.edu/Plato/republic.10.ix.html.

5. Ibid., book VIII, http://classics.mit.edu/Plato/republic.9.viii.html.

Gathering No Moss

1. Michel de Montaigne, "Of Repentance," in *Essays of Michel de Montaigne*, ed. William Carew Hazlitt, trans. Charles Cotton, https://www.gutenberg.org/files/3600/3600-h/3600-h.htm.

2. Ibid.

3. Ibid., "Upon Some Verses of Virgil."

4. Ibid.

5. Ibid.

6. Ibid.

7. Ibid.

Man Is a Hunting Dog Like Any Other

1. René Descartes, *A Discourse on the Method*, trans. Ian Maclean (Oxford: Oxford University Press, 2006), 51.

2. Ibid.

Growing Plants and Perfume

1. Baruch Spinoza, prop. XLV, "Part IV, Of Human Bondage, or the Strength of the Emotions," in *The Ethics*, trans. R. H. M. Elwes, http://www.gutenberg.org/files /3800/3800-h/3800-h.htm.

2. Charles Baudelaire, "Invitation to the Voyage," in *The Flowers of Evil*, trans. Keith Waldrop (Middletown, CT: Wesleyan University Press, 2006), 71.

Pedantry and Donkey's Milk

1. Françoise Gilberte Perier, *The Life of Mr. Paschal, with his Letters Relating to the Jesuits*, vol. 1, trans. W. A. (London: James Bettenham, 1744), xxi.

2. Blaise Pascal, fragment 5, section I, "Thoughts on Mind and Style," *Pascal's Thoughts* in *Thoughts, Letters and Minor Works*, trans. W. F. Trotter (*Thoughts*), M. L. Booth (*Letters*), and O. W. Wight (*Minor Works*), Harvard Classics 48, ed. Charles William Eliot (New York: P. F. Collier, 1910), 11, https://ia800708.us.archive.org/20 /items/Harvard-Classics/048_Harvard_Classics.pdf.

3. Blaise Pascal, letter XI, in *The Provincial Letters*, trans. Thomas M'Crie (Adelaide: University of Adelaide, 2015), https://ebooks.adelaide.edu.au/p/pascal/blaise /p27pr/.

Happiness in the Moment Is the Happiness of a Cow

1. Friedrich Nietzsche, *Untimely Meditations*, trans. R. J. Hollingdale, (Cambridge: Cambridge University Press, 1997), 59.

The Transitional Object

1. D. W. Winnicott, *Playing and Reality* (London: Tavistock Publications, 1971), 9.

2. D. W. Winnicott, "The Capacity to Be Alone," in *The Maturational Processes and the Facilitating Environment* (Abingdon, UK: Routledge, 2018), 30.

Learning to Understand Love by Watching Comedies

1. Stanley Cavell, Introduction to *Conditions Handsome and Unhandsome: The Constitution of Emersonian Perfectionism* (Chicago: University of Chicago Press, 1990), 18.

Animal Philosophies

1. See Friedrich Nietzsche, *Human, All Too Human*, trans. Helen Zimmern (Digireads.com Publishing, 2018).

2. Raphaël Larrère, *"Le loup, l'agneau et l'éleveur"* (The Wolf, the Lamb and the Farmer), *Ruralia* 5 (May 1999), trans. here by Jesse Browner. Thus, farmers who leave their sheep in the pastures and visit them but rarely do not meet their protection obligations under the domestication contract, and the wolf thereby assumes the role of scapegoat.

3. As proposed by Peter Singer in *Animal Liberation: A New Ethics for Our Treatment of Animals* (New York: New York Review of Books, 1975).

4. Blaise Pascal, fragment 418, section VI, "The Philosophers," *Pascal's Thoughts*, in *Thoughts, Letters and Minor Works*, trans. W. F. Trotter (*Thoughts*), M. L. Booth (*Letters*), and O. W. Wight (*Minor Works*), Harvard Classics 48, ed. Charles William Eliot (New York: P. F. Collier, 1910), 134, https://ia800708.us.archive.org/20/items/Harvard-Classics/048_Harvard_Classics.pdf.

INDEX OF AUTHORS CITED

A

Arendt, Hannah, 43, 44
Aristotle, vii, 35, 47, 48, 171–72
Artaud, Antonin, 14
Augustine, Saint, 75, 76

B

Baudelaire, Charles, 107, 142,
  189
Beauvoir, Simone de, 42
Bentham, Jeremy, 170
Bergson, Henri, 174
Blondel, Maurice, 70
Blumenberg, Hans, 105
Boétie, Étienne de La,
  52, 130

C

Callicles, 53
Camus, Albert, 29, 31, 54, 55, 175
Canguilhem, Georges, vii, 15
Cavell, Stanley, 197
Chrysippus, 45
Cicero, 176
Cioran, Emil, 124
Corneille, Pierre, 77

D

Derrida, Jacques, 24, 158
Descartes, René, 9, 22–23, 32,
  34–35, 37, 59, 65, 99, 100, 100,
  101, 116, 126, 171, 174, 186–87
Donne, John, 1

E

Elias, Norbert, 147
Engels, Friedrich, 86
Epictetus, 133, 134
Epicurus, 28, 54
Esquirol, Jean, 45
Evagrius Ponticus, 142, 143

F

Foucault, Michel, 170–71
Freud, Sigmund, 90, 146

G

Guyau, Jean-Marie,
  34

H

Hegel, Georg Wilhelm Friedrich, 51
Hobbes, Thomas, 85, 87
Horace, 139

I

Illich, Ivan, 34, 35

J

Jankélévitch, Vladimir, 158

K

Kant, Immanuel, 8, 93, 95, 116–17,
    117, 120, 123, 154, 156, 157, 161
Kierkegaard, Søren, 4, 8

L

Laborit, Henri, 131
Lafargue, Paul, 130
La Fontaine, Jean de, 96, 203
La Rochefoucauld, François de, 27, 168
Larrère, Raphaël, 199
Leibniz, Gottfried Wilhelm, 67–68
Leiris, Michel, 169
Levinas, Emmanuel, 23
Loyola, Ignatius, 143
Lucretius, 96, 98

M

Marcus Aurelius, 26, 50
Marx, Karl, 81, 102, 103, 116, 130
Melville, Herman, 177
Merleau-Ponty, Maurice, 11, 63
Montaigne, Michel de, 26, 27, 29, 52,
    69, 108, 124, 125, 125, 126, 167,
    168, 184, 185

N

Nietzsche, Friedrich, 3, 54, 72, 79,
    82, 82, 193, 199
Nilus, Saint, 143

P

Pascal, Blaise, vii, 29, 76, 78, 132,
    171, 176, 191, 192
Patočka, Jan, 39
Plato, vii, 53, 57, 63, 76, 95, 127, 127,
    155, 171, 181, 182
Porphyry, xx
Proust, Marcel, 71, 101

Q

Queneau, Raymond, 71

R

Racine, Jean, 46, 76
Ricoeur, Paul, 39
Rimbaud, Arthur, 51
Ronell, Avital, 56
Ronsard, Pierre de, 41
Russell, Bertrand, 160

S

Sartre, Jean-Paul, 66, 67, 67
Schopenhauer, Arthur 52, 53, 121,
    124
Seneca, 8, 48, 49, 50, 139, 142
Shakespeare, William, 48
Socrates, 6, 11, 12–13, 14, 23, 53, 154
Sontag, Susan, 35
Spinoza, Baruch 8, 54, 90, 91, 189

T

Thomas Aquinas, 123
Tolstoy, Leo, 175

W

Winnicott, Daniel W., 195

ABOUT THE AUTHOR

Graduate of the École Normale Supérieure, associate, doctor, and lecturer in philosophy Laurence Devillairs is a specialist in Descartes and philosophy of the seventeenth century. She is Dean of the Faculty of Philosophy of the Institut Catholique de Paris and is the author of *The Philosophy Cure* along with several other books published in French.